Early Days on the Upper Willamette

By

Veryl M. Worth

and

Harry S. Worth

REVISED SECOND EDITION

For the Benefit of

Oakridge Pioneer Museum

Dedicated to the Members and Volunteers of the
Oakridge Pioneer Museum
Oakridge, Oregon, USA

ACKNOWLEDGEMENTS

We want to thank those who shared their experiences with us for this informal history of our Upper Willamette area. We were pleased that a number of people responded to our newspaper request for biographical information.

We are grateful to Dorothy Holeman, Harry Clark, Bert Davis, L.L. Stewart, Artie Bouhey, Phyllis Julian and Michael Fisher, Editor of the Dead Mountain Echo, for all their help.

Library of Congress Catalog Number 89-085533
I S B N 0 942905 05 9

Copyright by Veryl M. Worth and Harry S. Worth
1989

Publisher and Distributor
FACT BOOK CO.
P.O. Box 601
Oakridge, Oregon 97463
503-782-2703

Printed by Koke Printing

Table of Contents

Chapter		Page
I	Beginnings	1
II	Indians of the Upper Willamette	3
III	The Lost Wagon Train	5
IV	Oakridge Yesterday	7
V	The Trappers	11
VI	Bynon J. Pengra and the Oregon Central Military Road	14
VII	The Railroad	16
VIII	Forest Rangers	23
IX	Logging and Lumber	28
X	Burial Grounds	45
XI	Early Post Offices	47
XII	The Early Schools	49
XIII	The Churches	54
XIV	Waldo Lake Irrigation and Power Co.	60
XV	City of the Upper Willamette	62
XVI	Medical and Legal Services	65
XVII	The Fish Hatcheries	67
XVIII	Newspapers	68
XIX	Memories	70
XX	Storms	72
XXI	Geographical Names	73
XXII	Resorts and Festivals	78
XXIII	Biographical Sketches	85
	Bibliography	130
	Index	131

CHAPTER I

Beginnings

The Upper Willamette community is endowed with a rich and colorful past, made so by the people who have lived here. There were those first pioneers, then came the trappers, ranchers, road builders, freighters, miners, loggers, lumbermen, construction workers, storekeepers, hunting guides, resort keepers, teachers, engineers, foresters, doctors, preachers, lawmen, outlaws, moonshiners, hotelkeepers, tavernkeepers, blacksmiths, railroadmen and dam builders, all with their housewives and children.

In 1853 the first great flow of pioneers crossed the Willamette Pass from Eastern Oregon following the middle fork of the Willamette river to the valley below. Over this route in the years that followed passed over 200 wagons, more than 1,000 persons and numerous herds of cattle. Some of these pioneers remained near what is now the city of Oakridge.

Today a handsome plaque stands in Greenwaters Park commemorating the "Lost Wagon Train," the first wagon train to make its way through the Willamette Pass.

The first permanent white settlers were the brothers James and Richmond Sanford who came in 1860 by pack train. James Sanford was born in 1831 in Richmond, Virginia, and came to Oregon in 1853. James, with his brother Richmond and their father Josiah, rode horseback across the plains to California during the Gold Rush. Then they came to Oregon in 1853 to look for a place to raise cattle. In 1860 they found the ideal place at Big Prairie and High Prairie on the Upper Willamette.

The three men owned nearly one thousand acres of land that was later to become the City of Oakridge, Circle Bar Golf Club, small ranches and home sites. Some of the land was homesteaded by the Sanfords and some was purchased from the Government. James was a cattleman and investor. He built the Sanford Building in Eugene. He never married. He died in 1913 and was buried at Pleasant Hill Cemetery.

James and Richmond had two sisters who came to Oregon. Susan Sanford Reed lived in California until the death of her husband and small children in an epidemic. She then came to Oregon and lived near her brother James. She, too, is buried at Pleasant Hill. The other sister was Lucinda Sanford Orr who was the mother of Theresa Orr, wife of Israel J. Gray, a pioneer of the Oakridge area. Lucinda was born in Virginia, died in Eugene and was buried at Pleasant Hill. (See *Biographical Sketches, Israel J. Gray* and *Thomas Orr*)

The Sanfords built the first building in what would become Oakridge. It was a log and shake cabin that they used as a way station. It was still standing when the railroad came to Oakridge. It was removed from the right-of-way so the railroad could be built.

The flow of settlers increased with the building of the Oregon Central Military Road, used as a route for freight wagons. For many years this was the only route over the Cascades in this part of the state. The Oregon Central Military Road was a direct route from the Willamette Valley to Fort Boise in Idaho. The road was completed before 1870, and it is now known as the Rigdon Road.

When freight wagons pulled by four- and six-horse teams were bringing supplies over the old road, Steve Rigdon had a stop where he furnished horse feed, housed travelers, sold groceries, and kept a tavern. Rigdon Road and Rigdon Guard Station get their names from Steve Rigdon.

The boom was on when Southern Pacific Company started the building of their railroad line in 1909. Work on the Natron cutoff linking Eugene and San Francisco ushered in a construction boom when hundreds of people came to work on the project. Oakridge was a natural site for a railroad subdivision point.

Before 1912 the town was called Hazeldell and after that time the name changed to Oakridge. The name Oakridge was suggested by Major R.L. Edwards, a right-of-way agent for the Southern Pacific Company. It accurately described the topography and the surrounding timber cover.

With the coming of railroad construction, E.T. Templeman moved his store from Westfir to Oakridge to become the city's first business operator.

Before Templeman started his store, the only store in eastern Lane County was the Hyland store at Lowell. Hyland had a post office and a general store. An account book of the A.D. Hyland store is one of the treasures of Lane County history.

In most Oregon stores of that day, people paid their store accounts with labor or produce such as eggs, fruit or smoked venison hams. The stores stocked patent medicines, such as Dandelion Tonic, Spirits of Nitre, Bitters, Camphor Gum, Hood's Sarsaparilla, Medical Discovery, Vermifuge and Halls Balsam. They also carried powder and caps, lead and primer, coal oil and wicks, ropes and nails, calico and buttons, as well sox and overalls.

Soon after Templeman moved his store to Oakridge, other businesses were started. E.E. Smith had a general store, Arch Wood and Grant Hyland had hotels and Sharp and Michael's established a livery stable.

By 1912 the railroad track was laid to Oakridge and people began to come from other places to stay at the local resorts and to hunt from such lodges as the Bear's Den. Local residents could get back and forth to Eugene much easier by train than over the rough, muddy road that linked them to the valley before the coming of the train.

During the Prohibition in the 1920's, there were moonshiners working in the hills above Oakridge. They packed corn and sugar to their stills or "cans" by pack horse until the revenue agents got too plentiful. Then they were forced to use more devious routes and carry the supplies on their backs. The whiskey was sold in gallon jugs and quart jars for twenty dollars a gallon. The moonshiners who were caught paid five hundred dollar fines and spent six months in jail. Some of the old stills have been uncovered in recent years by ranchers who now farm the land on which the stills were operated.

Businesses, homes, churches, schools, parks and much more have been built in Oakridge in this hundred years and more since the Sanford brothers first settled here. The development of the city, providing services to over two thousand people, was no small task.

Many of the men who have played a large role in the development of the area were with the United States Forest Service. These men were in every way trailblazers.

CHAPTER II
Indians of the Upper Willamette

Most of the Indians who lived in or passed through the Upper Willamette country were Calapooias (Kalapuyan), Molallas and Klamath. The Calapooias lived in this area in small groups of about 20 persons. Sometimes, with visitors, the groups would number a hundred or more for a short time. There is evidence that they camped in areas we now know as uptown Oakridge, High Prairie and Airport Road.

Indian artifacts found in the Upper Willamette area include obsidian arrowheads, rock scrapers, metates (flat table-like stones), Manos (hand rollers used for grinding) and mortars.

The Indians would hunt game and gather blackberries, huckleberries, salalberries, acorns and camas. They crushed acorns into flour. They steamed and then dried the camas root. The camas tasted like sweet potato.

Soon after the white settlers came to the banks of the Willamette, it became a custom of the Klamath Indians to come over the Willamette Pass each fall to pick hops in the hop yards near Lowell. On this annual trek, the Indians would buy deer hides from the white people and sell the gloves and moccasins they had made from deer skin.

In 1855, the Kalapuyan Indians ceded the Willamette River area to the United States Government and the Grand Ronde Reservation was set aside for them. By 1905, disease had killed all but about one hundred and thirty of the tribe.

There was a Mollala Indian named Charlie Tufti who lived with the Warner family. It is said that he and Frank Warner gave Salt Creek its name in 1887. Tufti Mountain is named for Charlie.

On April 21, 1884, Charlie Tufti was awarded legal claim to public domain at the General Land Office in Roseburg, Oregon. The homestead certificate number was 1687 and the application number was 2729. The general description of the land on the deed was as follows: one hundred and sixty acres of township number twenty-one, on the south range R3E, Section 1421 of Willamette Meridian.

On February 22, 1889, Charlie Tufti and his wife Lucy sold the property to Almanza C. McClane for $640.

It was unique for an Indian to be able to homestead land. In order to do so they had to set up residence separate from any tribe and adopt habits of civilized life.

After Charlie sold his land he moved to Warm Springs Reservation where he served the tribe as their chief.

There was another Indian named Jim Chuck Chuck who also managed to homestead land east of Oakridge.

Fortunately, there were no great Indian wars on the Upper Willamette such as occurred in Southern or Eastern Oregon.

Through the Cultural Resource Management Program of the U.S. Forest Service, over 150 archaeological sites have been found in the Oakridge District. Most of these are small scatters of stone tools and flakes of obsidian, a volcanic glass found in various locales of the Cascade Uplands and Central Oregon. The many small sites and ancient trails represent temporary hunting, stone tool manufacture and food gathering activities. We have four known rockshelters (caves) that were used by these ancient peoples on the Oakridge District, and there are a half dozen rockshelter sites on Rigdon District to the south. Rockshelters are very important because they preserve human cultural remains so well due to their dry conditions. We have learned much about the various peoples who have lived here and how their way of life has changed over time.

Research suggests that the area was inhabited seasonally for over 7,000 years with possible winter village sites in the vicinity of present-day Oakridge. Originally their hunting was done with atlatls (spear-dart throwers) using darts tipped with finely crafted obsidian, chert and jasper points. In the last 2,000 to 3,000 years, the atlatl was slowly replaced by the bow and arrow. Plant foods like camas bulbs, berries and acorns made up a large part of the diet. Grinding stones, cedar baskets, earth ovens, bone and wooden eating utensils made up their "kitchens." Fish, like trout and salmon, were caught by various means and were smoked and dried over fires for later use. Busy warm weather months were dominated by food gathering, travel and trading; winter was a time for togetherness, ritual, religion and storytelling while living off foods collected over the spring, summer and fall. Their way of life, though very different from ours, was likely dominated by some of the same trials and tribulations, wonder and happiness, good times and bad. In many ways, they left their mark on the landscape around us, contributing much to our own history and culture.

Current efforts by the Forest Service and professional archaeologists have two broad goals: To study and analyze prehistoric data to learn more about the Native American's adaptation, both social and technological, to the mountain environment; and to locate, manage and protect a very fragile public resource, our nation's cultural heritage, in the best way possible.

University of Oregon Museum of Natural History has a display of items from the Horse Pasture Cave, an archaeological site in the Upper Willamette area.

CHAPTER III
The Lost Wagon Train

The first Oregon immigrants to bring wagons through the Willamette Pass of the Cascade Range were the people of the Lost Wagon Train. They had left the east in eager expectation of obtaining free land in the fertile valleys of Oregon and of reunion with friends and relatives who were already settled in that distant land.

This was a large wagon train. A partial list of the families that made up the wagon train includes: Buckenhams, Cline, Elliot, Love, Miller, Parker, Parvin, Stevenson, Stewart, Warner and Williams.

John Stewart had his wife and three daughters with him. His daughter Agnes Stewart kept a diary recording most of the long trip. Some excerpts from the diary run as follows:

March 16, 1853 Leave Alleganey City, Pennsylvania.
March 25 Arrive St. Louis, purchase supplies.
April 9 Arrive St. Joseph, Mo. Bought oxen.
May 3 Leave St. Joseph. Travel 310 miles in 27 days.
May 31 Pass Fort Kearney.
June Near Black Hills, N.D. Stopped to rest the oxen because many of them had sore hooves and many were lame.
July 4 Celebrate by dancing.
August 26 Camp at Boise River. Many oxen and cattle have died.
September 8 In Oregon. Some families decide to take a short cut west through the Cascades. The others leave today to go by way of the regular route to the Columbia and then down the Willamette Valley.

The Stevensons and Buckenhams said goodby to Agnes Stewart and her family who intended to go directly west across the Cascades. Agnes stopped writing in her diary after they left the Malheur River and got to what she refers to as "very serious hills." The wagons were east of the Cascade range searching for the pass.

Then, according to the Charley Williams story told to him by his relatives who were descendants of members of the Lost Wagon Train, the westbound wagons traveled west and north so they were, for a time, on the Deschutes River.

In the train was a Captain Miller who had crossed the Willamette Pass on his way east to get his family. He had hoped that a road had been put through the pass since he last was there. However, this had not been done and the people in the wagon train were forced to build one or make a passage as they struggled through the mountains.

As they worked their way along, they threw away everything they could possibly do without. They left wagons, tools, household goods and even things that would be in short supply in the valley they hoped to reach. It was evident that if they were to reach the valley alive, they had to travel as lightly as possible.

Time after time they crossed the Upper Willamette, finally coming to Big Pine Openings on the west side of the Cascade Range. By now they had only a few head of cattle and oxen. The oxen were exhausted, the men were worn and anxious, some children were sick, the women were tired and one of the women was due to have a child.

Some of the men, in an attempt to find assistance, set out for the valley. Meanwhile, however, word that the wagon train was trying to cross the mountains had reached the valley, possibly carried by families who had taken the other route, and help was on the way.

Diamond Peak, wagon train and Central Military Road went south of this mountain.

Among those who went to the rescue were: Squire Powers, Cornelius Hills, Dan Hunsaker, Elixis Miller and John Parker. They arranged to transport the people most in need of care to Dexter or Lowell on horseback. The others were helped in getting the wagons down to the valley. Some of the families built homes at Dexter and Lowell and later one of the Warners made his home in Oakridge.

Through their fortitude, the people of the Lost Wagon Train made a valuable contribution to Oregon history. They blazed a trail over which many wagon trains would follow.

CHAPTER IV
Oakridge Yesterday

The evenings of September 8th and 9th, 1984, more than 450 people per evening packed the Oakridge High School auditorium to see the play, *Oakridge Yesterday*. Over one hundred people participated in the production of the play about the history of the Upper Willamette area.

Turning back pages in a small slice of Upper Willamette history infused a feeling of enthusiasm and pride among many members of the community, particularly those who brought the drama to life. It was living history which caught the imagination of young and old alike. The audience gave standing ovations for both nights' performances.

Of course, the appearance of Grammy and Emmy award-winning writer, composer, musician Mason Williams and his musician friends had a lot to do with the enthusiasm. Mason grew up in Oakridge, so he took time to come home and help with *Oakridge Yesterday*. He also had made a trip home in 1969 to do a concert for the Tree Planting Festival.

The play production coincided with the 50th anniversary of the incorporation of the City of Oakridge. The focal point on stage was a scenic mural of the town's mountainous skyline, done by Oakridge artist Carol Frederickson and assisted by Carol Clark. Mary K. Helikson and Veryl M. Worth were co-producers of the play, assisted in many ways by their husbands, Dale Helikson and Harry Worth.

The Program
OAKRIDGE YESTERDAY

Oakridge High School Auditorium
September 8 & 9, 1984

HISTORICAL DRAMA

Sponsored by the Upper Willamette
Pioneers Association

This project has been made possible in part by a grant from the Oregon Committee for the Humanities, an affiliate of the National Endowment for the Humanities, and also by a grant from the Oregon Arts Commission and by the National Endowment for the Arts.

Playwright . . . . *Dorothy Velasco*
Music . . . . *Mason Williams*
Historians . . . . *Gary (Joe) Searle, Louise Wade*
Master of Ceremonies . . . . *Dr. Ken Carver*
Director . . . . *Keith Putnam*
Stage Manager . . . . *Rachel Spencer*
  Assisting . . . . *Doty Spencer*
Co-Producers . . . . *Mary K. Helikson, Veryl Worth*

MUSICIANS

Mason Williams	Guitar
Billy Oskay	Fiddle
Mark Schneider	Bass
Art Maddox	Piano

CAST

Jasper Hills	Norman Oakley
Flora Hills	Mary Ellen Holly
Hallie Hills	Nomi Tonsgard
Lawrence Hills	Shane Henry
Eldon Templeman	Ronald Crandall
John McClane	Richard Beasley
Jessie Brock	Gyneth Prouty
Roy Beamer	Scott Cramer
Square Dance Caller	Don Iverson
Louis Flock	Don Hampton
Lina Flock	Rachel Spencer
C.B. McFarland	Bert Davis
Auctioneer	Ralph Perigny
Woman at Dance	Alene Hadley
Man at Dance	Marshall Mikesell
Foreman #1	Edwin Hadley
Foreman #2	Joe Goddard
Square Dancers	Acorn 8's Club
Caboose	Nancy Goddard
Children	Cris Snuggerud, Phillip Delong, Sasha Delong

ACORN 8'S SQUARE DANCERS

G.D. & Liz Collins, Edna Temple, Faye Alexander
Wes & Karon Tiller, Ray & Esther Clark, Paul
Daphne & Dustin Tiller, Ed & Alene Hadley, Jim & Ruth Jones
Marshall & Betty Mikesell, Eric Payne, David & Candy White

Sound	Garth Skaar
Lighting	Gene Shamek
Costumes	Phyllis Dentel, Alene Hadley
Makeup	Sandy Schroeder, Donna Redding, Bev Campbell, Tracy Krueger
Scenery	Carolyn Frederickson
Assisting	Carol Clark
Cut-outs	Harry Worth
Prompters	Elizabeth Tonsgard, Aline Goddard
Publicity	Cheryl Smith
Posters	Debbie Gillespie
Party for Press	Pam DeLong, Joyce Knight, Elena Fisher
Ushers	Marge Walborn
Pre-Show Exhibits	Dorothy Holeman

A SYNOPSIS

In order to enjoy and appreciate this play, it is necessary to mentally turn back the clock of time. All of the characters were people who really lived here, and the events portrayed really happened. So far as we know, only two of the people in the play are still living: Hallie Hills Huntington and Lawrence Hills.

Rather than a play, as such, with a plot, this presentation documents a series of events that took place in this area between the years 1908–1934. It begins with the decision of Jasper and Flora Hills to move up to this beautiful mountain area. There is a family discussion that includes the story of Grandfather Cornelius and his gold, along with other events like the Lost Wagon Train.

The next people to be introduced are store keepers Eldon Templeman and John McClane. They did not get along well, and after one particularly serious disagreement, actually did saw their store in half!

With the next appearance of the Hills family, discussion centers around the building of a hunting lodge and the coming of the railroad. Hazeldell becomes Oakridge in 1912. Then, Flora reminisces about the life of Jessie Brock and her marriage to Roy Beamer.

One of the two big community events portrayed is the New Year's Eve Celebration. While waiting for the square dance caller to arrive, people sit around in small groups talking about various things: the Crescent Lake monster, Jasper's new home, and politics. Louis Flock makes his first appearance in this scene. When the dancing does begin — upstairs in Templeman's store — it almost shakes the building down, and people are sent shivering outside.

(END OF ACT I)

ACT II opens with the relating of more ways progress continued in this area, such as the coming of the automobile and the beginning of Westfir. The story of the Crescent Lake Monster is more graphically presented when Lawrence Hills, Louis Flock and Lina Flock go out on the lake on a raft.

C.B. (Big Mac) McFarland was a very well-known man in this area. He served as Forest Ranger for 37 years from 1909, when Willamette National Forest was Cascade National Forest, until his retirement in 1946. One of the interesting stories he tells is how he, with the help of Forest Service personnel, made a man of a delinquent boy.

Mr. McFarland's story is followed by other human interest stories as recalled by Flora, Hallie and the rest of the Hills family.

The next scene is another large community affair, an old-fashioned Fourth of July celebration with all the trimmings — "Miss Columbia," a box social, a three-legged race and a pantomimed baseball game are highlights of the day.

Though these were by no means the only individuals and families who played a part in the development of this area, their experiences do present a good overview of how Oakridge grew.

All of the foregoing scenes were brought to life from the past — as if these people had returned to earth for a short visit in order to tell their stories. So, it is fitting that the closing scene has Flora and Jasper walking slowly off stage, wending their way back to eternity.

Ercle Ramey

Mary Ellen Holly plays the part of Flora Hills in "Oakridge Yesterday."

CHAPTER V
The Trappers

From the time the first settlers arrived on the Upper Willamette, there were trappers setting trap lines to catch the fur bearing animals. Almost every farmer did some trapping. After the animal was caught and killed, it had to be skinned. Then the pelt was stretched and dried on a board. Trapping was hard work even when game was abundant.

Bill McMahon and Harley Cain with cougar hides they took winter of 1936 — Photo courtesy Phyllis Julian.

One of the larger trapping expeditions carried out in the mountain country above Oakridge was the Paddock-Dompier trap lines of 1911–1912. Charlie Paddock and Frank Dompier built camps in five locations and ran trap lines from them. Their area of operation included Waldo, Maiden, Gold, Crescent, Clear and Odell Lakes, as well as Upper Salt Creek. They used handmade skis and snow shoes to get from place to place in the snow.

These two men trapped marten, ermine, mink, badger, raccoon, rabbit, bear, weasels and fisher (largest tree traveling animal). They set cat traps and caught lynx, civit cat and skunk, and they shipped large quantities of furs to the East that winter. Paddock also sent animal heads to Salem in lots of ten for an animal survey the State of Oregon was making.

The timber wolf, fisher, marten and cougar are now very nearly extinct. In 1910, they were plentiful.

Dompier and Paddock first met at Devil's Garden near Fort Rock. After they got to know each other and decided to become trapping partners, they bought their provisions and pack horses on the east side of the Cascades where they were living at the time. Some of the pack animals were later killed and used for trap bait.

Charles Paddock with catch of marten hides, winter of 1912.

Photo courtesy Paddock Family.

While they ran the trap lines at the high lakes, they sometimes made trips to Hazeldell (now Oakridge) to buy food and to visit. They must have liked the area pretty well because they both lived here most of their lives. Frank married a local girl, Flora Warner, the daughter of Frank Warner. Charlie went east to get his girl, Beulah Worden who lived in New York. It took him years to talk her into coming west with him.

Fred R. Sankey was one of the government trappers who came to the area at the request of a rancher who had a band of sheep in the mountains. Wolves had killed 54 head of sheep. Sankey came in August 1930 packing over Staley Ridge to a camp near Skipper Lakes. He trapped and killed a number of wolves. One of them weighed 98 pounds. Fred Sankey was later a trapper supervisor.

Louie Kotch was another old time trapper that Paddock and Dompier often visited on their trips to Hazeldell for supplies. Kotch Mountain is named for him.

Ernie Hebert did quite a lot of trapping and hunting. He took beaver, otter and muskrat from marshy areas. Ernie had a reputation as a good woodsman and tracker. He was most active in the 1920's and 30's.

The Oakridge Museum has pictures of other trappers such as Leo McMahon at Brock cabin, D. Lynes at the Hoy Ranch with Frank Dompier and a Mr. Singletary with some large bear hides in 1919.

Frank Dompier and another trapper with their marten catch, 1911 at Odell Lake, snowshoes in the snow.

Frank Dompier and Charles Paddock, trapping partners, 1911.

Photo courtesy Oakridge Museum.

CHAPTER VI

Bynon J. Pengra and the Oregon Central Military Road

The Oregon Central Military Road and the man responsible for its being built, Bynon J. Pengra, had an important effect on the development of the Upper Willamette area. He and his associates made the original surveys for the wagon road transversing the Cascades which ran through the Willamette Pass. This group of men also made possible the financing of the road.

In 1970, this sign was on the Old Military Road southeast of Oakridge — Photo from Worth Collection.

The Civil War and the Indian Wars were in progress and the settlers of the Willamette Valley needed a supply road from Boise, Idaho, over which supplies and firearms might be moved to western Oregon.

Shares at $250 each were sold to raise the sum needed to build the road. The Federal Government granted the company of shareholders every odd-numbered section to a distance of three miles on each side of the road. In this way, the Government helped to get the much needed supply road built. B.J. Pengra was in charge of the construction. The work began in 1864 and was completed in 1867.

The sections of land given the shareholders were later sold and resold many times.

Pengra was appointed Surveyor General of Oregon in 1862 by President Abraham Lincoln. Before he became Surveyor General he was the fiery editor of the People's Press, a Republican anti-slavery publication in Eugene. Pengra's paper had a battle of words with M. Ryan who was the principal of Columbia College (the forerunner of University of Oregon) and a writer for the Democratic Herald, a competing newspaper. Pengra's paper was anti-slavery while the Herald and Ryan were pro-slavery.

Ryan finally hit the boiling point and on June 22, 1860, he armed himself with a pistol and went looking for Pengra. He found his man in Elsworth and Belshaw's Drug Store. Ryan fired, but missed. Pengra then grabbed Ryan by the throat and was choking him when spectators pulled him off. Ryan fled both the scene and the area. It is believed that Ryan went to Virginia where he joined the Confederate army.

The Oregon Central Military Road made the Upper Willamette area much more accessible. Owners of some of the shareholder land grants transformed their acreage into farmsteads on the Upper Willamette. Some built cabins and lodges where they could go to hunt. The road was one of the greatest factors in the development of the area.

Pengra Pass, located in the Cascades just west of Odell Lake and presently used by the Cascade line of the Southern Pacific railroad, was discovered by and named for Pengra. W.H. Odell and B.J. Pengra visited the pass in July, 1865.

Pengra and his wife Charlotte Stearns Pengra came to Oregon over the Oregon Trail in 1853. B.J. Pengra died at Coburg, Oregon, in 1903.

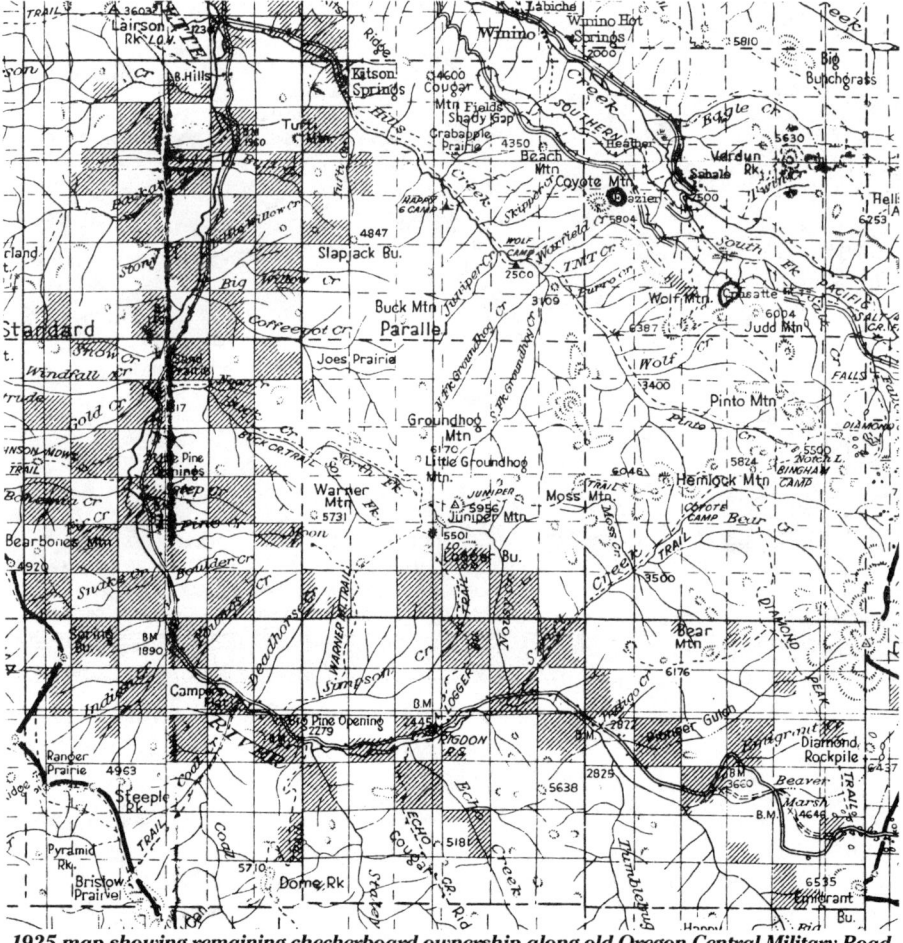

1925 map showing remaining checkerboard ownership along old Oregon Central Military Road.

CHAPTER VII
The Railroad

September 1, 1926, the Cascade Line of the Southern Pacific Railroad was ready for traffic. A crew was ready to take engine 3703, a 2-10-2 steam engine with freight cars, up the hill. They left Eugene soon after two in the morning and reached Abernathy late in the day, too late for the crew that started with the train to take it on over the pass. The uphill grade had forced them to take on water every few miles to keep the steam engine going, and these delays had taken more time than anticipated. Another crew had to take over at Abernathy as the men were not permitted to work longer than a 16-hour shift.

Steam shovel and dirt train at work during construction of the Cascade Line, working east of Oakridge, 1926 — Photo from Southern Pacific Historical Collection.

On that first run for the summit, W.L. (Bill) Tupper was the engineer and Robert (Bob) Tracy of Oakridge was the fireman.

The 270-mile Cascade line between Natron, Oregon, and Black Butte, California, opened to freight and local passenger traffic in September, 1926, and to all through traffic on April 17, 1927. It provided a route that was 25 miles shorter and had a lower grade and fewer curves than the original line over the Siskiyou mountains, which was built in the late 1880's.

Construction of one part of the railroad had been started in August of 1909 at Natron, near Eugene, and the line, referred to as the Natron cut-off, was open to Oakridge in May of 1912. The other part of the line, from California to Kirk, Oregon,

41 miles north of Klamath Falls, was also opened in 1912, leaving an unfinished span from Oakridge over the pass to Kirk.

Resuming work on the Cascade Line (Natron Cut-Off), earthmoving by horse power, 1923 — Photo from Southern Pacific Historical Collection.

Work was resumed on this 108-mile gap in September of 1923 and was finished in the summer of 1926. From then on and throughout the early 1930's, as many as five passenger trains each way passed through Oakridge. From the time they first had service in 1912, people of the Upper Willamette made great use of train travel.

From 1926 to 1954, there were station operators at stations all along the Cascade line — at Fields, McCredie Springs, Wicopee, Cruzatte, Cascade Summit and Crescent Lake. There were also operators at stations between Natron and Oakridge. They copied train orders and then gave them to engineers as the trains passed their station. When it was necessary for two trains to pass, they held the trains at the station, so that one train could go on the siding. Since 1954, that work has been done by electronics. The engineers can tell what to do by lights along the railroad.

Andy Draper, who was station agent at Oakridge, copied the last order at this station, ending the old system.

The station agent keeps records of cars on hand, ordered and furnished. He sees that freight cars move as needed to and from local mills.

Helper engines go with trains as far as Cascade Summit, then turn around and come back. The extra engine-power is needed to get the trains over the mountains.

There used to be a one-end tunnel at Cascade Summit. It was built because there was not sufficient space for engines to turn around. By backing into the one-end tunnel, the engines were able to about-face. Present day engines go back and forth without the need to turn.

The old engines had to have the cab forward of the power source so that the operators would not be overcome by the smoke and heat, especially when they went through the tunnels. The engines that had the cab back of the power source caused a lot of grief for the operators.

Oakridge had a round-house at one time, with stalls for two engines. Although it was called a round-house, it was square in shape. No matter what the shape and regardless of the railroad term, a round-house is a garage for engines.

The road master and road crews are the people who keep the tracks and road-bed in good condition so that trains can travel without danger. A road master is stationed at Oakridge and he has many crews that work in the area.

In 1943, there were 14 scheduled passenger trains daily, seven each way, all stopping in Oakridge.

Both Edna Temple, who lived at Cascade Summit, and Frances Hill, who lived at Wicopee, rode the trains from the high country to Oakridge. Many of the families who lived near the railroad came and went by train, and children went back and forth to school by train.

King Klamath Falls and Queen Eugene are "married" on the tracks of the completed Natron Cut-Off, 1926 — Photo from Worth Collection.

During the heyday of these trains, passengers could get off the train at Diamond Creek, take the three-quarter-mile hike down a trail, view Salt Creek Falls, then return home by the next train. At that time there was no highway near the falls as there is now.

The railroad depots of Westfir and Oakridge are long gone. Oscar Frederickson was a long-time station agent at Westfir and Andy Draper was at Oakridge.

The late Richard L. Neuberger wrote an article that was published in the Saturday Evening Post about the rotary snow plows that keep the Cascade line open in winter.

Melvin Bristow, a descendant of Elijah Bristow of Pleasant Hill, was a Southern Pacific road master at Oakridge. Many of the men who worked on the trains and the road of the Cascade line have come to live on the Upper Willamette.

The railroads demanded that railroad men have watches that had at least 21 jewels and the watch had to be inspected at least once a year by a certified railroad watch inspector. Perry A. Ashcraft of Oakridge was a certified watch inspector for many years and many of the railroaders working through Oakridge took their timepieces to him to be checked.

Derailment of helper engine at Abernathy, fall 1940 — Photo courtesy Dorothy Holeman.

1964 Record Floods Ravage the Railroad

Violent storms began sweeping in from the Pacific a week before Christmas. These storms, continuing for 21 days, combined with unseasonable melting of the snow pack in the high mountains, brought widespread destruction to the West Coast and caused record damage to SP railroad facilities in Northern California and Oregon.

Damage to Southern Pacific lines was in excess of $5 million. Worst hit section of SP was near Cascade Summit (elevation: 4,885 ft.) in Oregon where all train operations on the main route between San Francisco and Portland were halted for 18 days.

In the pre-dawn hours of Tuesday, December 22, against the roar of a 68-car freight train moving westward over the Cascades from Oakridge to Crescent Lake came another sound — that of an avalanche of timbers, rock, mud and snow. Down a ravine toward Tunnel 14 at Frazier, the avalanche roared, smashing into the train and carrying five cars to the bottom of the canyon. Shortly afterward, another slide came down the ravine, triggered by the sudden release of accumulated runoff that had broken through one of the dams of debris far up on the mountainside. With it disappeared 100 feet of mainline track and roadbed.

Station at Cascade Summit, winter 1940 — Photo from Worth Collection.

A thundering earthslide swept away 130 feet of a 300-foot steel bridge at Noisy Creek, 20 miles north of Crescent Lake. At Salmon Creek, near Oakridge, a mountainslide slipped down, covering 700 feet of track with mud and whole trees to a depth of 60 feet.

While SP forces on several work trains tried to clear the line, there came still more slides, causing serious damage to bridges as the rains continued in full force. The rampaging waters of Salt Creek, which wiped out some 25 miles of parallel Oregon Highway 58, also undermined the footing of SP's long steel viaduct, and only heroic efforts of SP crews to divert the waters prevented collapse of the structure.

The fast dispatching of work trains to trouble spots early in the storm left workmen in strategic locations in the mountains, despite the numerous blockages that quickly followed.

With the slides and washouts in the Cascades came trouble elsewhere. Rising flood waters caused other washouts on SP lines in the Willamette Valley and over the Siskiyou Mountains.

Some 300 feet of mainline track north of Albany, between Eugene and Portland, were washed out, although SP's westside branch bridge across the turbulent Willamette River held fast to permit the rail evacuation on Christmas Eve of some

200 persons from North Albany. There was also a special run across the bridge to help save a sick child in need of emergency hospital treatment.

Slides and high water on highways isolated the town of Oakridge and for a time the only access was by rail from Eugene for supplies of water, food and medicine.

Three vital bridge spans to replace the 130-foot gap in the slide-damaged Noisy Creek Bridge were made at SP's Sacramento General Shops in a marathon effort involving more than 3,800 man-hours of work in three days.

Already on hand at the shops before the emergency were some big bridge girders needed to form the sides of the spans, but these had to be cut to size and tied together with many criss-cross structural members, each requiring over 70 bolts.

Because the Noisy Creek Bridge curves slightly as it crosses a 90-foot-deep ravine some 20 miles north of Crescent Lake, Oregon, the spans required many hours of detailed design work. The curvature also complicated construction problems.

Work was started on Christmas Eve and it continued around the clock until 7 p.m. Sunday, December 27, when two 50-foot and one 30-foot span were loaded onto flatcars for their journey north.

Train just came in to Oakridge depot, 1913 — Photo from Oakridge Museum Collection.

About 65 men were on duty during the three days, including boilermakers, blacksmiths, machinists, sheetmetal workers, carmen, painters, electricians, draftsmen, laborers and supervisory people. Hot meals were sent in and gallons of coffee consumed. The men stayed on the job until it was finished, many working 12-hour shifts.

Called back from retirement to help with the project were V.R. Cooledge and R.S. Bennett, former engineer and assistant engineer of bridges, respectively.

G.P. Nagtegaal, engineer of structural design, and bridge designer M.B. Chan, both of San Francisco, also helped guide the work.

"It was quite an undertaking," says W.O. Brown, superintendent, of the Mechanical Department's Northern District, "requiring cooperation of men from all the various crafts. It was one of the finest examples of teamwork I've ever seen."

Southern Pacific placing girders on Shady Creek viaduct on June 12, 1926, during construction of the Cascade Line — Photo courtesy Southern Pacific Historical Collection.

During World War Two, there were many stations along the railroad between Springfield and Crescent Lake. They were: Springfield Junction, Carter (Minow), Reserve (siding), Armet, Westfir, Tunnel, Oakridge, Pryor, McCredie Springs, Wicopee, Fields, Frazier, Cruzatte, Abernathy, Cascade Summit, Odell Lake and Crescent Lake.

At each of the stations there were telegrapher clerks on duty to give train orders to each passing train. Many of those jobs were filled by women during the war. Women also worked in the roundhouse and the sandhouse in Oakridge.

CHAPTER VIII
Forest Rangers

The tools of the trade for a Forest Ranger at the turn of the century were a horse, a saddle, a gun and a badge. The pay was $60 per month and the Ranger furnished his own horse and saddle. Addie L. Morris was appointed Forest Ranger of the General Land Office by the Acting Secretary of the United States Department of Interior, Thos. Ryan. He was a Ranger in the Upper Willamette area from 1899 to 1905. His duties included patrolling, game warden, surveying, erecting cabins, trail building, timber marking, log scaling, locating sites for mills and hotels, fire fighting and being a deputy U.S. Marshal.

The 1899 Ranger Station at Big Prairie and pictured are A.L. Morris, Ranger, and his wife and family. The tent was used for visiting friends — Photo courtesy of U.S. Forest Service.

Morris built two cabins at a location where Southern Pacific has a tunnel at Westfir. They were referred to as twin cabins.

A portion of his diary reads: October 1, 1901 Left camp at 7:A.M., started across to McKenzie trail, to Belknap Springs. Arrived Brock cabin at 4:30, distance traveled 30 miles. October 4, 1901 Left camp horseback at 7:00 A.M. and started to find trail in fog, hunted till 10:30, found trail, traveled 20 miles to Horse Pasture, camped, no feed, distance 25 miles.

The first two years Morris was in the area he brought his family here for the summer and he stayed alone in the winter. Then after 1901 his family stayed the year round.

Morris was the son of George Jackson Morris of Harrisburg, Oregon, and his brother was Joseph Henry Morris.

When the management of forest land transferred from the Department of Interior to the Department of Agriculture, Morris chose not to accept his transfer.

Cy L. Bingham was another Ranger appointed by Acting Secretary of the Department of Interior, Thos. Ryan. Cy also had to furnish his own horse and equipment, and he too received $60 per month. His appointment was effective June 1, 1903. At that time the area was divided so that from 1903 to 1905 Morris and Bingham each had a separate area to work in.

1940's photo of Claude Jones, Oakridge Ranger who retired in 1921, and C.B. McFarland, Oakridge Ranger from 1924 to 1946.

With the coming of the railroad and the mills, there was a greater and greater demand on the forests of the region and a greater and greater need for personnel to manage the timber lands, so that the Ranger Districts have had to grow to meet those demands made on the forest lands both for timber and recreation use.

From 1924 to 1946, Corley B. McFarland, often called "Big Mac," was Ranger of the Oakridge District and he held that position longer than anyone else who had been Ranger at Oakridge.

Mac was Ranger at a time when telephone lines were being run to criss-cross the forests with a communication system used for fire control. These were the days of the mountain top look-out towers, and fire crews that moved by horseback or on foot.

It was quite common then as it is even now to refer to any man in a forest service uniform as a ranger or forest ranger although only the head man in each Ranger District is the Ranger.

When Jasper and Flora Hills operated a hunting lodge near the site of Hill's Creek dam, Flora made this notation in her diary: May 5, 1913, Good day but warm, Lawrence and I are here alone until evening. Rangers Mr. Dunning, McFarland, and Roy Flock came for supper and breakfast, putting up telephone line for Rigdon place.

Before C.B. McFarland was Ranger at Oakridge District, he was a Ranger at large and at one time he and his wife Ruth lived at the West Boundary station located in an area now covered by the waters of Lookout Point Reservoir.

Trail crew back of Buckhead Mountain, 1913. There are two Tiller men, Roy Flock and others.

After his retirement in 1946, he and his wife Ruth moved to their ranch a mile north of Oakridge. McFarland died at his home on June 17, 1969. The McFarlands had two sons, Harvey and Lee. Mrs. McFarland was the daughter of Grant Hyland who owned the Oakridge Hotel in 1909. She was the granddaughter of early day Lane County store owner A.D. Hyland.

After the management of the forest transferred to the Department of Agriculture, the Rangers of the Oakridge District were as follows: Martin S. Durbin 1905–1908, John Hill 1908–1909, Charles T. Beach 1909–1911, James L. Furnish 1911–1913, Claude R. Jones 1913–1921, Roy O. Parks 1921–1923, J.F. Campbell 1923–1924, C.B. McFarland 1924–1946, William Cummins 1946–1958, Stanley Undi 1958–1961, Alvin Sorseth 1961–1965, A.L. Warren 1965–1967, Ormond H. Doty 1967–1974, Wayne E. Orr 1974–1979, Robert L. Barstad 1979–.

From 1908 to 1947, Rigdon was in the Oakridge-Salt Creek Ranger Districts. The Rangers of the Rigdon District have been as follows: Robert Mealey 1947–1947, Ivan W. Crumb 1947–1949, Otto B. Hannell 1949–1956, Gordon S. Sanford 1956–1959, W. David Kolb 1959–1963, Michael D. Lysne 1963–1976, Robert L. Barstad 1976–1979, B. Eric Morse 1979–1982, Herb Wick 1982–.

Salt Creek Ranger District: Ralph E. McCurdy 1959–1961.

Some of the major forest fires that have ravaged the Upper Willamette area were, Dead (Green) Mountain — 1898, Dead Mountain — 1910, Waldo — 1910, Oakridge — 1917, Brock — 1919, Coffee Pot — 1919, Koch — 1919, Salmon Creek — 1919, Kelsay Ridge — 1945, Kitson Ridge — 1946, Pryor — 1952, Emigrant Butte — 1955,

Paddy's Valley — 1955, Fields-Wicopee — 1957, Pryor — 1960, Sinker Ridge — 1967, Captain Prairie — 1967, Dead Mountain — 1967, Shady Beach — 1988.

Ranger McFarland referred to Dead Mountain as the "bogie" of the Oakridge Ranger District (due to the fact that it had burned so many times and would have burned more if small fires had not been suppressed so quickly).

Ranchers who lived on the mountain or near the mountain have suffered losses from the Dead Mountain fires. A fire in 1883 burned the homes of Mr. Allen and James Ashley and animals were lost on the ranches of Jim Sanford. In a later fire, the William Reardon ranch suffered losses.

When Dead Mountain burned in 1910, a crew of men who were building the railroad tunnel west of Oakridge helped get the fire under control and a rain came on the 21st of September to finish the fire.

The old lookout towers or cabins are fast becoming a thing of the past but for forty years or more they were part of a great fire control network. A towerman, or in some cases towerwoman, would take a two-week supply of groceries and pack in by horse or jeep to the lookout located on a high peak in the forest. Water usually had to be packed from the bottom of the peak or further. The cabins or towers were glass on four sides and it was a part of the job to keep the glass spotless.

The lookouts were equipped with phones or radios for fire reporting and for regular reports to headquarters. The towerman could order his next supply of food by phone or send it with someone who had visited the tower. The supplies would be taken to him by packer.

When a fire was spotted, the towerman would locate it on his round map fire finder and communicate the location to headquarters. Then he would set off with a pack of tools to try to put the fire out before the other crew arrived at the fire.

Bill Minick and his pack train in Devils Canyon on the Brock Trail.

Towers and cabins were equipped with lightning rods to lessen the danger of damage by lightning, which is inclined to strike the tops of mountains. During lightning storms the smell of ozone was heavy around some of the lookouts.

The job once done by the towerman is now done by air patrol.

All the Rangers of Oakridge, Rigdon and Salt Creek Ranger Districts have left an imprint on the Upper Willamette area. Almost all have started new programs for fire control, reforestation, recreation and cultural resources. As more demands are made on the forests, more ways are found to handle the demands.

As a tribute to some of the rangers there have been recreation sites, creeks, forests and roads named for them.

One ranger in particular has left a legacy to the young people of the area. Claude R. Jones, Oakridge District Ranger from 1913 to 1921, died on November 23, 1968, at the age of 90. In his will he left a scholarship fund that amounted to $120,000 in 1970 and amounts to $500,000 in 1989.

Any student of the area who wishes to continue their education beyond high school can borrow from the fund at a low rate of interest. The one stipulation that was strongly expressed in the will was that the applicant must not have been convicted of a misdemeanor or a felony.

The fund will be a perpetual source of assistance to worthy students of Oakridge-Westfir area desirous of obtaining higher education, either academic or vocational. The fund is not limited to students with high scholastic rating. Mr. Jones believed strongly in education. He helped establish the area's first high school.

CHAPTER IX
Logging and Lumber

The following article was written by Paul Ehinger, Jr., for an English class at Oakridge High School, June 8, 1966. Will James was the teacher of the class. The article, slightly edited, is used with the author's permission.

AUTHOR' S NOTE

The information for this paper was gathered from the files of the Edward Hines Lumber Company's Westfir Division. The information concerning the death of Bill Ferrin came from interviews with Clarance Hebert and Tack Larwood conducted by Chuck Lowman.

The reasons given for the poor financial showings for the mill under the Blythe, Witter, and Company were the opinions of Bruce Hoffman, who made a report on the Westfir mill for the Hines Lumber Company prior to the purchase of the mill by Hines.

This is only a brief sketch of the history of the mill. More could be learned by interviews with men associated with the early days of the mill. Different sources within the Hines files disagree on dates. The dates found in this paper are the ones that either agree or are more reasonable in the light of known facts.

—Paul F. Ehinger, Jr.

Westfir — The Mill

In 1923, the United States Forest Service put 685 million board feet of timber up for sale. This timber was located along the drainage of the North Fork of the Willamette River. The contract for the timber specified that a "stable community be established to provide decent living conditions and to encourage family life." The agreement also required the contractor to construct a logging railroad up the North Fork at a cost of almost $1.7 million. At the time of the sale, the Forest Service expressed a desire to develop "opportunities for a permanency in a well-balanced lumber operation." With this statement, the Forest Service assured the purchaser of the timber sale a continuous supply of 50 million board feet of timber a year to keep the mill in operation.

The timber sale was purchased by the Western Lumber Company on July 22, 1923, for $1.50 a thousand board feet of timber. This company was founded and run by George Kelly. Kelly was a logger whose experience dated back to the days of logging with oxen. During the First World War, Kelly served as a Colonel in command of the Forestry Batallion of the 20th Engineers in France. Many of the men who were later to work with Kelly in Westfir also served in the Forestry Batallion. Kelly's family had a lumbering background. By this time, his brother John Kelly was a partner in the Booth-Kelly mill in Springfield.

The mill at Westfir was designed by Captain Starbird, a man who served with Kelly during the War. Construction on the mill began in the summer of 1923. Starbird was in charge of the construction of the mill.

A small mill was constructed upstream and across the river from the site of the main mill. A dam was built across the river to form a log pond for the small upper mill. The small mill was built to cut lumber for use in the construction of the main mill. A short time after this mill was built, it was destroyed by fire. Lumber for the main mill was brought in by train after this happened.

Records show that the total construction time for the mill was approximately two years. Construction was completed on May 31, 1925. The mill was designed to produce almost two hundred thousand board feet of lumber a day. This is about 50 million board feet of lumber every year. The mill began regular operations on the day after construction was completed, June 1, 1925.

In 1924, a dam had been constructed to make a log pond for the main mill. During the winter of 1925 this dam was washed out. The dam which had been built for the short-lived upper mill was used for log storage while a new dam was being constructed for the main mill.

The Western Lumber Company ran into financial difficulties soon after its founding. Kelly had been assisted in his finances by Herbert Fleischaker of San Francisco. Difficulties required that they secure loans from various banks. The reason for these financial troubles is not known. It is possible that the construction of the mill and the town cost more than Kelly anticipated. Finally, in either 1925 or 1926, the company was forced to issue bonds. The major buyer of these

Steam Donkey on sled. Harley Cain in center back row — Photo courtesy Phyllis Julian.

bonds was Blythe, Witter and Company. When the Western Lumber Company began defaulting on the bonds in 1928, Blythe and Company converted the bonds into income bonds under California laws and took control of the Western Lumber Company.

Shortly after Blythe took control, the operations at Westfir were given new management. Blythe and Company appointed Myron Woodard of Silver Falls Lumber Company general manager of the entire Westfir operation. Woodard in turn put his son-in-law Bill Ferrin in the position of resident manager at Westfir. Ferrin took charge of the operation directly from George Kelly. Some time after becoming manager, Ferrin inspected the old upper dam, which was now of no use. While he was trying to decide what should be done with the dam, he fell to his death. A small forest camp on the old route of Highway 58 between Westfir and Oakridge was named Ferrin Forest in his honor. The upper dam was blown out in either 1935 or 1936.

Even with the change in management, the mill failed to make a profit during the time Blythe and Company owned it. Finally, in the latter part of 1935, a "Bondholders Protective Committee" was formed. By a series of financial moves, the bonds held by Blythe and Company were converted into stock and purchased by Blythe with the bonds. With this move, the Western Lumber Company was dissolved and became the Westfir Lumber Company, a division of Blythe and Company.

However, even after this reorganization, the operation at Westfir failed to show a profit. They were able to pay off debts they had incurred, but could show no profit. It seemed that this was a poor place to have a mill and that it was impossible to make it a paying proposition. However, a great many of the financial problems of the mill could be explained by poor management. The management of the mill didn't look and plan for the future. They were always out to cut as much as possible as fast as possible to make a quick profit for the banks and stockholders. As a result, no roads were built for access to timber ahead of the time it was needed. In some winters, the mill almost had to close down because there was no more accessible timber. The timber at lower elevations didn't have roads to it. The Forest Service had to bail the company out of trouble during the winter more than once. To keep the mill running, the Forest Service found low level sales for the company so that the mill wouldn't have to close down for three or four months during the winter.

Westfir logging incline used to lower logs from Huckleberry Flat to the railroad on the North Fork — Photo from Oakridge Museum collection.

Finally, in 1944 after failing to realize any profits, Blythe decided to sell the Westfir Mill. Edward Hines Lumber Company became interested in the mill because it wanted a supply of Douglas fir lumber. However, Hines already had one mill in Oregon which was entirely dependent on government timber and the company was unsure that it would be wise to obtain another mill dependent on government timber. Hines consulted with the Forest Service which said that it would be happy to have a responsible company like Hines control the operations at Westfir. The Forest Service was unhappy with the utilization practices of the Westfir Lumber Company.

In August 1945, the Edward Hines Lumber Company purchased the mill at Westfir from Blythe and Company for approximately two million dollars. Immediately after taking control of the mill, Hines began a program of modernization. In 1951, Hines built a modern plywood plant at Westfir at a cost of more than two million dollars.

North Fork, pond, dam and mill at Westfir.

After the plywood plant began production, employment at Westfir soared. This was the peak time of employment.

Some of the Hines office people who are well remembered are: Carl Wester, auditor and office manager; Norman Husser, chief accountant; M.R. Grundeman, personnel and safety director; Norman Stone, manager until 1951; Bee Bernard, Stone's secretary; Howard Lemons, manager (he and his family drowned in Dexter Lake auto accident); Paul Ehinger, manager and vice president; James Anthony, manager; and Beverly Woolridge, secretary to manager.

Postscript

After that, employment dropped each year due to modernization of the plants. By 1969, Hines at Westfir had about 430 employees. The trend of automation continued and cost of timber continued to escalate.

By 1977, the plants had 340 workers and were having problems keeping the plants up to DEQ standards. Hines sold the plants to Mitchell, Blacketor and Associates of Medford, Oregon. They then leased the plywood plant to Westfir Plywood Corp.

The plant operated a short time and then a series of fires destroyed the sawmill, veneer plant and plywood plant.

By 1988, all that remained of a once thriving lumber cummunity was a small store and post office, a few homes and a picturesque wooden bridge over the North Fork. Reforested hillsides and a beautiful river will keep homeowners in the area if they are retired or have employment elsewhere.

North Fork Logging

The mill at Westfir operated a logging railroad up the North Fork to about a mile above Tumble Creek. Camp 5 was located there. At one time there were about 180 men staying at the camp. There was no road into camp but the railroad. Men and supplies all came in by rail.

The mill had three steam locomotives — a 1926 Willamette, a Baldwin and a Shay. The heavy Willamette was the best according to Roy Knapp and others who worked on the railroad.

An engineer, a fireman and two brakemen made up the crew. The brakemen set and released the car brakes and handled the switching as well. One brakeman rode in the engine and the other rode in back of the train. If the need arose, they walked the logs on the cars of the moving train.

Doug Dick and spool of wire rope at logging supply.

Veryl Worth photo

Logs on North Fork, on way to mill pond. Old bridge and railroad bridge in distance.

The engines were fueled with a thick oil. It was so thick it had to be heated before it would flow, so the engines were kept fired all night. The fireman had to fire up the engines at 10:00 P.M. every night. They had real problems in cold weather.

The engines took on water at Westfir and at Camp 5. A boxcar was used to haul groceries to the camps.

The logging railroad up the North Fork operated from the late 1920's until the tracks were removed in 1952. At that time, the railroad was replaced by the regular road for truck and auto use. The road was built on the old railroad grade.

An incline was part of the logging railroad system used at Westfir. It was a unique one that gained national attention in its day. It was standard railroad line that went straight up the side of a mountain. Nearly halfway up the slope, the track divided. Two lines ran the rest of the way to the top. The system worked somewhat like a pulley. When one car went up the hill, another one went down.

At the top of the incline sat one of the most powerful snubber donkeys men could build. Specially constructed for the job, it sported such logger's delights as a double extension fire box, a nine-foot bull wheel, two nine-foot brake drums, bands lined with oak blocks that were internally cooled, a low gear for heavy hauling, Westinghouse locomotive air power controls, and an automatic dial to tell the operator (called the donkey puncher) where the carriers were located on the incline.

The donkey was used to pull the cars up the incline, but more than that, its job was to slow down, or hold back, the loaded cars going down the hill.

At the top of the hill was Huckleberry Flat logged in the 1920's and early 1930's. Westfir Mill's railroad lines ran over the flat and on High Prairie.

The cars to haul the logs and the locomotives came to the area by way of the incline. There was about 10 miles of track going into the logging shows.

The heaviest load that the donkey had to pull was the fuel for the locomotives. In order to get the heavy oil tank car up the incline, the snubber had to pull the

Old Westfir dam and fish ladder. New dam, built after 1964 flood took old one out, did not need fish ladder because of Dexter Dam.

tank car half way up, take a breather to get up steam again, then pull the load up the rest of the way.

Once in a while a load of logs broke away, running to the bottom of the hill where it would end in the river bed.

Camp 3 and Camp 6 were on the top of the hill above the incline while Camp 5 was further out on the North Fork. If all was going well, the incline could move five loads of logs an hour, for a total of 500 thousand board feet of logs each day.

Lumber loading docks at Westfir before 1950.

For many years Wilbur Winfrey loaded the logs at the top of the incline and Walter Blakely ran the incline donkey.

Huckleberry Flat was reforested by a combination of natural regeneration and planting by the Civilian Conservation Corps (CCC) in 1936. Robert "Hop" Dunning, who worked for the Forest Service, was foreman of the planting crews on the flat. There are remnants of the old logging railroad in the area but they are hard to find. The new trees have taken over and are growing tall.

EARLY LOGGING

Whether he logged in 1875 with oxen or now with modern equipment, the contract logger is about the same sort of man. He has to have a lot of determination. He stags his jeans and wears suspenders and calked boots as well as many hats, for he's a financier, engineer, forester, road builder, negotiator, equipment operator, mechanic, purchasing agent and whatever else he has to be to get the logs out of the woods.

In 1875, a man named Packard logged for a time in an area above Deception Creek. He took out some Sugar Pine logs that were over four feet in diameter. The trees were felled with axes and hauled to the river by oxen then shoved in the river and driven to the mill in Springfield. The pine logs were so heavy that many of them sank and did not make it to the mill.

Poleyard west of Oakridge railroad depot, 1918 — Photo courtesy Oakridge Museum.

In order to use oxen for logging, it was necessary to keep them well shod as their cloven hooves had very thin shells. The iron ox shoes had to be replaced often.

Logs were driven from the Upper Willamette area to mills downstream from 1875 to well after the turn of the century. The logs would be logged and decked on the river banks during the winter then driven down river in the spring. A crew of four men would make the drive. A cook also went along and prepared meals along the river banks. Grace Hills Walker cooked for her father's log drives. The river men were paid three dollars a day, which was double what they were paid in the woods for a ten-hour day.

Dee and Hal Russell with log truck, 1919 — Photo courtesy Oakridge Museum.

At the turn of the century, stumpage was 25¢ per thousand board feet. Some of the men who logged at that time were Joe Carter, Charlie Williams, Jasper Hills and George Larison.

In 1905, Jasper Hills was logging in the Grays Creek area with horses and about this time he purchased a steam donkey which is believed to be the third steam donkey Willamette Iron and Steel made. The first donkeys did not alter logging procedures greatly but as soon as the logger started lifting the front ends of the logs in the air, he began to make progress and move the logs with greater ease.

Moving the Booth Kelly donkey boiler to Fall Creek. Mr. Firman driving the eight horses — Photo courtesy Lawrence Hills.

Steam logging donkeys became a common sight at early day logging operations. A large sled built of logs, an upright steam boiler, a steam engine and cable winch drums made up the machine. It was capable of moving from one site to another by hooking a cable to a large tree. As the cable wound around the drum on the donkey, the sled would move toward the tree.

As diesel and gas engines became available, the methods changed. Now portable towers are moved through the forests from site to site on heavy, motorized trucks.

More men came to log in the 1920's, 30's and 40's. John Orr took cedar logs from Box Canyon in the 30's. These logs were hand cut and horse logged. The crew included Luke and Jim Rogers and Ernie Hebert.

Earl Walker cut cedar poles from Crowbar Point, drove them down river to Oakridge, then shipped them by rail from there. This was about 1920. In the 1940's, Earl and his son Donald had a sawmill and they logged for their own mill on High Prairie. By this time, a lot of the loggers had tractors to log with as well as high-lead equipment.

There was a logger here named Bill "Bull Pine" Faust. Before he was a contract logger, he was a faller and bucker. Some of the other men who have logged the Upper Willamette at one time or another are Mex Raines, Luke Rogers, Jim Rogers, Bud Long, Ted Bedell, Bert Davis, Eddie Roberts, Wallace Neal, Swede Gibson, A. Carter, Jack Rardin, Howard Towne, Harding Brothers, Galla Logging Co., McDougal Brothers, Al Crist, Joe Dugger, Wilbur Hyland, Y.B.Y. Corp. (Young Brown & Young) and Jim Whitaker.

A few of the men in the early logging crews were: Walt Holt, Bill Puckett, Claude Hardin, Ed Eaton, Wes Wilhelm, Wesley Shackleford, Bill Ross, Roy Cain, Charlie Pettijohn, "Dude" Bedell and Clay Parker.

Booth Kelly log drive on the Willamette at Jacoby farm area. Driver of team is Lester Jacoby. Bill Eaton sitting on log — Photo taken by G.E. Jacoby, Worth Collection.

Since the late 1960's, there has been some balloon and helicopter logging in the Upper Willamette area.

Logging supplies came from the lower valley until 1966 when Melvin Mckinney and Douglas Dick opened the Oakridge Logging Supply. Doug Dick became sole owner in the early 1970's.

POPE & TALBOT, INC., AND THE PENN TRACT

On July 2, 1946, after a great deal of study by Loran L. Stewart, Chief Forester, and other Pope & Talbot managers and Board of Directors, the Penn timber tract was purchased.

An interesting side line to this tract of timber perhaps is a little history of the ownership. The original grant was to the Oregon Central Military Road Company for constructing the road from the Willamette Valley to Eastern Oregon where it hooked up with other military roads. The grant was for every other section three miles either side of the road.

The Booth Kelly Lumber Company purchased the land from the summit of the Cascade Mountains to the Willamette Valley in the very early 1900's. Of course, there was no transportation. The railroads weren't built then, so there was no active management of the land. About 1911, the Penn Timber Company purchased the land from Booth Kelly. These people were from Pennsylvania and their name was Wheeler. They also owned the Portland Telegram Newspaper. Jasper B. Hills, who lived above Oakridge on the Middle Fork, was caretaker for the Penn Timber people for many years.

Taxes mounted up and with no demand for timber this organization went into bankruptcy. It was in the courts for many years and Max Tucker, President of the Cascade Plywood Company of Lebanon, Oregon, managed to gather up the bonds and get the title cleared. His purpose was to exchange this so-called Penn timber tract to the Forest Service for forest timber in the South Santiam Drainage. The counties blocked the deal because of the tax implications it had. Tucker then put the timber up for sale and Charlie Hines of the Hines Lumber Company who owned the mill at Westfir took an option on it for $1,750,000. He did not exercise his option and Mr. Lueddemann, Vice President of Pope & Talbot took an option for $2,500,000 with $100,000 down. This resulted in the sale to Pope & Talbot.

Pack string on Logger Butte trail, August 1947, taking supplies to camp for Pope & Talbot engineers — Photo courtesy Harry Clark.

It was estimated that one billion 100 million board feet of timber (Douglas fir and associated species) were standing on those lands, and in the same drainage there was about five billion board feet of Forest Service timber that could be harvested cooperatively.

Before the timber could be harvested, much engineering had to be done. The land had to be surveyed, roads constructed and timber sales laid out. Pope & Talbot also would be building a lumber mill at Oakridge.

They made use of the old C.C.C. camp at Oakridge where they set up a cook house and temporary quarters for logging and engineering crews.

Under the direction of Stewart, they began the engineering task. Harry Clark, Dick Behr, George Griffith and Frank Kincaid would drive to Rigdon Guard Station on the old Central Military Road, leave there with pack horses and camp gear and make camp where they would stay a week or ten days at a time. To cross the river, they used the old sheep bridge or cut logs to cross the river on foot.

At that time, there were about 400 people in Oakridge and very few telephones, with one long distance line to Eugene. The central switchboard was in Charlie Croner's drugstore, which was also the liquor store, and was only activated during the drugstore business hours. Mr. Croner asked $5,000 for his telephone system which probably was worth practically nothing, but he did have the telephone franchise in Oakridge.

While Hines Lumber Company was logging the North Fork of the Willamette River for their mill at Westfir, Pope & Talbot was opening up a whole new area for logging on the Middle Fork.

There had been very little logging activity south or east of Oakridge.

Pope & Talbot advanced $1,242,813 to reconstruct the Rigdon Road, which penetrated the Middle Fork watershed for 26.3 miles. The Forest Service issued Pope & Talbot a special-use permit to reconstruct the road to Forest Service Class CC Standards. The permit provided for (a) free use by the Forest Service; (b) free use by the general public; (c) use by other operators providing they contributed an equitable share of the cost. The Forest Service share was repaid to Pope & Talbot through timber sales over the next several years.

By the spring of 1947, excavation and construction for the sawmill and log pond had begun. By April 6th, 1948, the Oakridge mill was in operation and able to produce 200,000 board feet of lumber per eight-hour shift.

For the next 40 years, Pope & Talbot would be the mainstay of the Oakridge economy, having an annual payroll that exceeded one million dollars even in the first years of operation.

Through trades with the Forest Service, they acquired land that is now Green Waters Park. Pope & Talbot gave the land to the city for the park.

Pope & Talbot and the Forest Service have replanted the areas that have been logged during the years of operation in the area. Those lands are now a vast tree farm.

Camp at Wolf Shelter, August 1947 — Photo courtesy Harry Clark.

Sheep bridge across the Middle Fork of the Willamette, 1946. Harry Clark and friend — Photo courtesy Harry Clark.

Harry Clark crossing Willamette on log bridge, 1947, on way to camp — Photo courtesy Harry Clark.

Many managers and workers have come and gone over the past four decades, but Harry Clark, Chief Forester from 1958 until his retirement in 1986, was on the job at the start of Pope & Talbot, Oakridge operations in 1946.

Renovated CCC camp bunk houses used to house Pope & Talbot men until other housing could be built, March 2, 1947 — Photo courtesy Harry Clark.

Pope & Talbot, Inc. — The Oakridge Sawmill

The Oakridge mill was built on property once owned by the families of Melvin and Kay Spatz, Jack and Minnie Wright, Fred and Molly Hensen, Felix Dompier and the Hebert family.

The Pope & Talbot, Inc., ground breaking ceremony took place on April 22, 1947. Although the mill would open in less than a year, it was not an easy year for those who made it all happen. They worked through a very wet winter, in a raw and undeveloped area, with rains, snow, mud and floods making their work that much harder. The road builders, loggers, engineers and construction men did get the job done on time.

The following is a part of the news release by Pope & Talbot on the opening of the Oakridge project on April 6, 1948:

> From the start our company has cooperated with the City Council of Oakridge, with our officials working with them for the development of their city. Facilities at first were inadequate to house even the small group of workers laying the groundwork for the sawmill and log pond. After negotiations with the Forest Service we rented an obsolete CCC Camp very close to the millsite, which after renovation and remodeling, was ready for occupancy in March, 1947. The Camp houses some 120 men and is the site of the cookhouse. Various properties were purchased — these, together with new buildings, today offer excellent housing to employees either on a rental or purchase basis.

The rated capacity of the Oakridge mill on an 8-hour shift basis, is 200,000 feet. A total of 150 sawmill workers will be employed, with approximately 175 workers in the woods. The sawmill generally consists of a double cut band mill with horizontal resaw and pony edger. The plant will also have a small cant gang, and both a green and dry planer, with dry kiln capacity for the entire production, if necessary. The mill yard is of sufficient size to air-dry almost an unlimited amount of lumber. Six miles of the main logging road, from Hills Creek to Coffee Pot Creek, have been completed, with some 15 miles yet to construct.

The management would be very remiss if a few words of commendation were not written about the fine staff and their men, who have so diligently labored during these difficult months of major construction against many odds. Particularly, we mention the following:

W.N. Hammerschmith — who has so ably directed the construction of the sawmill, in addition to performing his duties as general mill superintendent at St. Helens and Port Gamble.

L.L. Stewart — who has co-ordinated these various phases of setting up an operation at Oakridge, in addition to working with the Forest Service on all phases of special use permits, timber sales and many items of mutual interest.

George Barnes — who has instituted a major logging operation, supervised road construction, mill pond construction, in addition to keeping his ever-watchful eye on other company logging operations.

W.J. Burgan — who has been Mr. Hammerschmith's right-hand man at all times in the construction of the mill, as well as in maintaining the mill at St. Helens.

Georges Bouhey — who has labored against shortages, delays, and other difficulties in rushing the construction adequate housing for essential workers.

Marion Heidrich — who has co-ordinated the logging operation and road construction, and operates the cookhouse. He is an able administrative assistant to George Barnes, General Logging Manager.

Carl Blakely — who has performed untiringly through all kinds of adverse weather conditions as the company's chief engineer. He has located logging roads, the railroad spur and bridge over Salmon Creek, the mill pond, water and ditch lines, supervised the construction of same from an engineering standpoint.

Lawrence Cook — who has been in charge of logging road construction, working against time and bad weather a goodly part of the last year.

A.M. Belyea — who has been timekeeper for the Oakridge operations and performed a most loyal and conscientious job, handling a multitude of detail which always follows the initiation of a new operation.

Pope & Talbot sawmill in operation, late 1940's or early 1950's — Dotson photo.

Over the years, a number of products were produced at the Oakridge site. In 1953, a product called "Fersolin" was made in a new plant at the mill site. The product was a soil conditioner. Georges Bouhey was plant manager.

Logger Butte lookout, about 1947 — Photo courtesy Harry Clark.

A particle board plant utilized shavings from the planing mill. In 1961, a veneer plant was added to process "white speck," peelable logs. Al Haynes was superintendent of the veneer plant.

In 1972, a complete new sawmill was built to replace the one built in 1947.

There have been thirteen resident managers at Pope & Talbot, Inc., Oakridge operation. They were L.L. Stewart, George Barnes, Art Brooks, L. Fuchec, Wayne Safle, John Snyder, Frank McPherson, Gail (John) Carver, George Ritchie, Robert Burke, James Anthony, Richard Woods and Roger Hayes.

The end of an era came in the summer of 1989 when the plant was sold to Bald Knob Land and Timber Company.

Building Pope & Talbot sawmill at Oakridge, July 20, 1947, burner foundation on the left — Photo courtesy Harry Clark.

Pope & Talbot sawmill and log pond at Oakridge.

CHAPTER X
Burial Grounds

The Pioneer Cemetery a few miles south of Oakridge on the hillside overlooking Hills Creek Dam is the burial ground of many early settlers. John Hill, for whom the cemetery is named, once farmed the land where the dam now stands.

Just how many are buried there and who all of them were is a mystery. The Upper Willamette Pioneer Association has worked hard trying to identify the graves. A few of them were marked but many of the markers had long ago rotted away. What records there are show the following persons were buried there:

Name	Burial Date	Name	Burial Date
John Hill	1906	Percy Winfrey	1898
John J. Ryker	1916	....Shelly....(Kicked by horse, Kitson Springs)	
Erma Jean Ryker			
Sam Ashley (born 1829)	1891	Alice Dennison	
Ida Ashley	1878	Bertie Calleman	
Cora Winfrey	1894		

Peter Hebert built some of the burial boxes. Earl Walker and Charlie McClane built John Hill's box.

Members of the Pioneer Association who have worked on the restoration of the old cemetery think there are more than 20 people buried there. Some 16 depressions were counted when members of the association cleared and surveyed the area. The cemetery was last used in the 1920's.

Other Burial Places

Before the turn of the century, many people were buried on their own land or in a burial plot on a neighbor's property.

There were graves on the William Walker place at Oakridge. These have been moved to Forestvale Cemetery.

Jim Sanford's father was buried on the old Sanford place but has been moved to the northwest corner of the Pleasant Hill Cemetery.

There is one grave on the Donald Walker place, that of William P. Allen who died in 1878.

Forestvale Memorial Park

When Peter Hebert, patriarch of the Herberts of the Upper Willamette area, was killed by a hit-and-run driver in Eugene in the year 1911, his son George had him buried in his favorite place. It was under two large oak trees on George Hebert's place. Other Heberts were buried nearby at a later date and the place was set aside for burial. As other families also wanted to be put to rest there, the Heberts gave the land as a cemetery.

Later the Grays, who were related to the Heberts, also donated land to the cemetery. Others may have sold or donated land for the cemetery.

A well at the cemetery was put in with money that was a memorial to William Hebert.

Retired Oakridge Ranger Claude Jones looked after the cemetery for many years. By the late 1950's, he asked the newly formed Upper Willamette Pioneer Association to look after it. Henry Holt was President of the organization, so he took over the job for a number of years.

A Cemetery Association had been formed and is still in operation. They have a President and a Board of Directors who look after the cemetery.

Anyone who owns a lot in Forestvale is a member of the Cemetery Association. Care of the cemetery is done through donations and with volunteer labor. All members are urged to go to the annual meetings and to help with the care of Forestvale. Raymond Clark is President of the Association in 1989. Forestvale Memorial Park is on McFarland Road.

CHAPTER XI
Early Post Offices

Date Established	Name of Post Office	Postmaster
1850	Skinner's	Eugene Skinner
1850	Pleasant Hill	Elijah Bristow
1868	Springfield	Albert Hovey
1872	Butte Dissappointment	Samuel Handsaker
1875	Changed to "Dexter"	
1873	Big Prairie (now Oakridge)	Addison Black
1882	Hill (above Oakridge)	John Hill
1883	Lowell	Amos Hyland
1895	Tiptop	Isaac Hamner
Prior 1910	Hazeldell (now Oakridge)	Anna McClane
	Hazeldell (moved to Hebert place)	Mrs. Bert Hebert
1910	Eula	Mrs. Blakely
1912	Oakridge	Mrs. Hebert
1914	Landax	Wilbur Hyland
1924	Winino	Vivian Cartwright
1926	McCredie Springs	Vivian Cartwright

(Winino and McCredie Springs were same location)

In 1909, the Post Office was located near where the Pope & Talbot mill now stands and the name of the Post Office was Hazeldell. The following names were listed in the Money Order Register of 1909: S.E. Walker, D. Dunning, Mamie Flock, Nelly Holt, Charles Hebert, Wm. Hill, Belle Warner, R.M. Holt, Roy Harvey, Peter Hebert, Mrs. G.W. Hamner, William Walker, Frank Warner, Wm. T. Kelsay, Walt Eddy, B. McDowell, Alice Holt, Thomas J. Gray, Grace Hills. Later some of these names change, some of the girls marry, Grace Hills becomes Grace Walker and Nelly Holt becomes Nelly Hebert.

Listed in the Register for 1910 are: Chas. Mardini, Geo. McMahon, C.D. Morgan, T.O. Russell, W.H. Wolf, James George, Arthur Wolf, W.T. Watson, L. Falkner, L.G. Koch, Mrs. T. Gray, I.I. Wiley, Robert Shimmin, Gus Freeland, T.J. Goodson, Lawrence Holland, Mrs. T.J. Robinson, W.L. Norris, E. Johnson, T.A. Cameron, L.L. Addington.

These Hazeldell residents of 1910 sent their money orders to such places as Sears Roebuck and Co., Chicago, Ill.; Montgomery Ward and Co., Chicago; Lipman and Wolf Co., Portland, Oregon; Meier and Frank, Portland, Oregon; John A. Salzer Seed Co., LaCross, Wis.; The Eugene Guard; Silver Lake Leader; Hyland Bros., Lowell, Oregon; Honeyman Hardware Co., Portland, Oregon; The Examiner, San Francisco; First National Bank, Portland; Oregon Journal, Portland; American Woman, Augusta, Maine; The W.J. Comstock Co. Ltd., Morristown, N.Y.; Wells Fargo Co., Springfield, Oregon; and Farm View Seed Assn., Syracuse, N.Y.

It would seem that they kept up on the news and planted quite a lot of seed as well as making other interesting purchases.

Sarah Strong Jones (Mrs. Claude Jones) was Postmaster of Hazeldell Post Office and the Oakridge Post Office when the name was changed. She held the position for 25 years.

The Star Route was first established in 1940. The first three patrons were Charles T. Beach, Oscar McAtee and W.W. Allen. Ross Starr was the first contractor for the route. He used a 1941 Plymouth car the first year. He had the route for about 30 years. The last years he carried the mail, his second wife Alma took part of the route because it had grown tremendously.

Evelyn Hansen worked at the Post Office when Mildred Blair was Postmaster. Evelyn worked with Rose Sims, Sarah Dunn, Jean Spellmire, Cris Schwebke, Maxine Drumm, Dorothy Reed, Judy Balander and Ross and Alma Star.

After Mrs. Blair came Fred Hays then Norman Jellum as Postmasters at Oakridge.

Some Westfir Postmasters have been Mrs. Stewart, Phyllis Ryman, Sarah Dunn, Lucile Carter and Jean Bucholtz.

STAR ROUTE SERVICE
ESTABLISHED IN 1845

U.S. Mail six-horse hitch.

CHAPTER XII
The Early Schools

Hazeldell and Oakridge

The first schools in the area were provided by the pioneers who had taken land here and felt the need to educate their children. They hired a teacher for as many months as they could afford to pay one and provided a place for the teacher and children to meet and hold school. The earliest schools were held only about three months per year; but as time went on, the school period became longer until it finally reached nine months each year. Most of these first schools had six to twenty children and one teacher who taught all grades.

This second school in the Oakridge area was located where Pope & Talbot mill pond is. Picture taken in 1909, Nellie Holt, teacher. All the kids were present that day. Photo courtesy Lawrence Hills.

One of the first schools was located west of the Oakridge Golf Course on what is now the Ed Allen place. In 1875, the first teacher was Elmira Reynolds. The next year, Ella Pengra, daughter of Bynon J. Pengra, was the teacher.

In 1895, a log schoolhouse was built on the V.F. Hebert property. This location was just south of the present Pope & Talbot log pond. By 1909 there were nine students in this school. They were the four Hebert boys, Raymond Dunning, Mick McMasters, Florence Holt, Flora Warner and Lawrence Hills. Earnie Mathews was one of the teachers at this school which, according to Lawrence Hills, ran about three months a year.

The 1911–12 year was a memorable one for Oakridge. Dora Hyland was the teacher for a six-month term; and with a school census of seventeen children, it became necessary to find larger quarters. Arch Wood was building a new hotel and the kitchen area was nearly enough completed to house the school children. Seated at crude desks, they listened to the sound of saws and hammers as they learned their three R's.

Oakridge High School as it was in the late 1940's.

In the fall of 1912, Hazeldell became Oakridge and the new school building on the hillside above First Street was ready for occupancy. It was a two-room building but was used as one large room until September 1919. The large jacketed stove was in the back of the room and, needless to say, the front of the room was generally cold in winter. Effa Fenton was the first teacher in the new building and the school census increased from twenty-one to fifty children that year.

C.H. Zevely taught the first nine-month school term in 1913–14 for a salary of $65 per month. Gladys Smith became the teacher for the 1914–15 school year and Hattie Van Vleet took over for the 1915–16 term.

The old hillside school, built in 1912, became the Legion Hall in later years and was used for Boy Scout meetings and Saturday night dances in the 1940's and 50's. Standing on land that is now used as a parking area for the funeral home, it was torn down in the 1970's.

The first high school in the area was located in a small storefront building. The year was 1919. By 1922 the class of seven students, all girls, included Vera Hills, Goldie Clark, Louise Walker, Eula Clark and Edna, Lillian and Katherine Ryker.

In 1924, a wooden structure was built on the site of the current grade school and was in use there until 1950 when it was moved to a site west of the high school. In its latter location, it was used as a junior high school until no longer needed and was then torn down. In 1929, a brick building was constructed on the site of the current high school. After having been remodeled and expanded twice, this building was finally torn down and replaced with the current school.

High Prairie

Prior to the fall of 1915, students in the High Prairie area attended school in the old Patrick place. Teachers taught for terms ranging from four to twelve weeks. In order of their service, the teachers included Mr. Hiett, eight weeks; Nellie Holt, twelve weeks; Frank Hutchins, who taught for thirty-one days in the fall of 1910 and sixteen weeks in the spring of 1911. Veda Barbre taught in the fall of 1911 and Nellie Holt Hebert taught in the spring. Malena Momb taught eight weeks in the fall of 1912.

Mr. and Mrs. C.H. Zevely, R. Laura Ruth and Kathleen Russell were the teachers in 1913 and 1914. It isn't surprising that the students don't remember the names of their teachers during those first years.

The High Prairie area was not growing as rapidly as Oakridge and in November of 1914 only three names, Thelma Chenoweth, Leo Blanton and Clair Hamner, were added to the school census. Despite slow growth, the school was relocated from the Patrick house and eventually consolidated with Oakridge in 1934.

The students of 1916, with Edna Holcomb Michael as teacher, included Carl, Amy, Dale, Clair and Ruby Hamner; Boyd, Pearl and Alta Wolf; Hazel Hebert and Thelma Chenoweth. Some of the teachers that served in the final years were Edna Stephens (1915), Fanny Stewart (1916–17), Clara Irwin (1917), Clara Prokop and Hazel Leith (1918–19), Candace Dillard and Alice McBee.

Other Communities

Landax School, 1904. Back row: Teacher Albert Neet, Clara Clark, Walter Blakely, Grace Walker, Bessie Kelsey, Harvey Cain. Middle row: Maude Cain, Vina Kelsey, Iva Cain, Ferril Cain, Beulah Cain, Letha Kelsey, Millie ---, Laura Sharp, Hallie Hills, Harley Cain. Front row: first two unknown, Clayton Kelsey, Roy Cain, Wilbur Winfrey. Photo courtesy Phyllis Julian.

There was a log schoolhouse on the Winfrey place located near the site of the second railroad tunnel west of Oakridge. This school operated from 1899 to 1903. Some of the students were Sam and Eva Morris; Ivy, Nelly and Crate Holland; and Ivy and Roy Cain.

Several small communities and schools once flourished along the Middle Fork of the Willamette River. Old maps show Landax and Blakelyville between Lowell and Oakridge, but the sites of these communities were covered by water when the Lookout Point Dam was built.

The school at Landax in 1911 had children from the Winfrey family, Ruth Hyland, Clayton and Letha Kelsey, Laura Sharp, and Edith and Elsie Cain, as well as others we have not been able to identify.

There was an old log school near Lowell named the Middle Fork School. In 1905, Mary Blakely was teaching there with a class of sixteen students. In 1973, Mary Blakely and her eight surviving students held a reunion. Those who came back after sixty-eight years were Siegle Tiner of Dexter, Dan Winfrey of Eugene, Sid Stiers of Lowell, Edna Tiner McMasters of Dexter, Stella Blakely Baxter of Eugene and Clara Stiers Sagersa of Kelso, Washington.

Westfir School, 1934. First grade teacher Esther Siefken. Back row: Richard McGee, unknown, Myrtle Stonebreaker, unknown, Kenneth Johnson, unknown. Middle row: Richard Stonebreaker, Jimmy Anthony, Eileen Lansberry, Phyllis McMahon, Dale Tuchardt, Freddy Swanson. Front row: Dorris England, unknown, Melvin Powell, Neil Long, Billy Foster, unknown, Eldon Powell, Vernon Hapner. Photo courtesy Phyllis Julian.

A boxcar, standing on a railroad siding, was used for the school at Cruzatte, which is a station on the Southern Pacific line about fifteen miles above McCredie

Springs. The school was for the children of the men working on track, tunnel and snow shed maintenance for the railroad.

Class size ranged from nine to fourteen and teacher pay included a two-room apartment, fuel and transportation of groceries from Eugene or Oakridge. Salaries ranged from $85 to $105. The afternoon passenger train slowed down enough each day to put off mail, papers and fresh milk.

During the winter of 1934–35, there was snow from late October to late May, with the deepest undrifted snow measuring 120 inches. There was no way to get above Oakridge by road in winter, but in summer and fall Cruzatte could be reached via the old Central Military Road.

Lawrence Moffit was County School Superintendent while Cruzatte School was in operation, and Joyce Stephens and Susan Broadbent were two of the teachers who taught there.

Oakridge School, all grades, 1923. This school was located between First and Second Streets on Ash Street.

CHAPTER XIII

The Churches

First Baptist Church

The Oakridge First Baptist Church began as a home mission project in 1945 in the home of Henry Wilcox, Jr. The group met every week for Sunday School and worship.

The evening meeting for young people was held in the Westfir Community Church. The average attendance was 23. An Easter banquet the following spring was attended by 60 young people.

In 1947, visiting pastors conducted services in the Seventh Day Adventist building on School Street.

A lot was purchased in 1948, a building was erected in 1949, and the first services were held on Sunday, May 7, 1950 — without benefit of a roof.

The present sanctuary was dedicated in 1961, and other additions were made in 1973.

Damascus Baptist Church

The Southern Baptist Mission was organized in 1954 under sponsorship of Trinity Baptist Church, Springfield. Services were held in the American Legion Hall for the first four years with Ray Runyon as pastor.

In 1957, they had services on their own property on East First Street. They were organized into a church in 1958 with the following charter members: Sue Cook, Ruby Barton, Ron Barton, Harry Cook, Lloyd and Ellen Cook, Russell Barton, Dean Cook, Alfred Dillard, Levi and Effie Edie, Max and Ann Pettit, Eddie Pettit, Alva and Wanda Rodgers, Mack Smith and Florence Lane.

In 1968, the church purchased seven lots on Spur Avenue. In 1974, the property on East First was sold and a church was built on the Spur Avenue property. The first service in the new church was on March 30, 1975.

The following pastors served the church in Oakridge: Ray Runyon, Max E. Pettit, Carl A. Walker, Earl Lowen, Bob Craig, Carl Webb, Jr., Dewayne Thompson, John Myklebust, John T. Davis, Joe Mays and Everett Stockton.

The First Christian Church

Prior to 1933, the First Christian Church of Oakridge held meetings with evangelist Teddy Leavitt in the Strand Hall on First Street. Student ministers also came to town to fill the pulpit.

The first regular minister was Anor Emerson, who worked full time at the Joe Crahan sawmill, and called on his church members after work.

For a short time the church members met in the old theatre building. Then in 1933, they started a real church building. Jim McGillvrey hauled the first load of lumber for the construction.

When the church was first built, there were from 50 to 60 young people attending services. The church provided recreation for the young people including many picnics and a party every Saturday night.

The 1933 building has been replaced by the handsome present one, finished in September 1966.

Open Bible Standard Church of Oakridge

The Open Bible Standard Church of Oakridge was started some time before 1926 through the efforts of Mrs. Frank Warner. Meetings were first held in the homes of Randolph Holt, Raymond Dunning, L. Howard of Oakridge and the Rev. Stanley R. Humphrey of Westfir. The latter was the church's first minister.

From 1926 until 1935, members met in the Strand Hall at Oakridge. Then in 1935, the church on First Street was built.

Besides the Rev. Humphrey, other early day ministers of the church were the Reverends Greer, McIntire, Greyell, Lawton and Anderson.

Members of the Frank Warner family and the Stanley Humphrey family who founded the church were descendants of John Stewart, a member of the "Last Wagon Train," whose daughter, Agnes Stewart, recorded the events of the long trip to Oregon. Agnes Stewart was the first teacher in Springfield, Oregon, and perhaps she started a family tradition by serving as a missionary as well as a teacher. Agnes also taught Sunday school for Indians at Fall Creek where she lived for a time.

Assembly of God Church

Since about 15 members of the Assembly of God Church began holding services in 1948 under the leadership of Rev. Marshall Faulk, the church has shown a pattern of steady growth. Services began in the home of Rev. Faulk, then moved to a store building where they were held until the present church on Highway 58 was completed.

In 1955, the church officially joined the fellowship of the Assemblies of God.

The parsonage was built and ready for occupancy in 1963, and the sanctuary was remodeled in 1964.

St. Michael's Parish

Catholic history in Oakridge-Westfir dates back to 1921 when the Catholic Church Extension Society sent St. Peter's Chapel car and Father Eugene McGuiness to give a series of Catholic instructions.

By 1937, there were a few Catholic families in the area, the John O'Connell, Louis Streit and Joseph Yunk families among them. By 1938, a Father Leipzig was having monthly Mass alternately in the American Legion Hall in Oakridge and the Community Club in Westfir. In Westfir the confessional was behind the organ. Another unusual feature was that while the priest was saying Mass, the fragrance of coffee and bacon cooking came temptingly from the cook house into the "Chapel."

By 1940, an Alter Society was organized. Among the officers were Mrs. John O'Connell, Mrs. Louis Streit, Mrs. F. Whittaker and Mrs. C.R. Elliot.

When they decided to build a church, Louis Streit was appointed chairman of a building committee. Other members were: Virgil Caskey, A.E. Gerimonte, John O'Connell, L.D. Blodgett, A. DuMont and W.G. Sutton.

They found the ideal building site on a knoll in Oakridge and the ground was purchased from Claude Jones for one hundred dollars.

The Catholic Extension Society of Chicago donated $2,500 toward the new church on condition it be completed in 1941. It was completed on time and dedicated on August 3, 1941.

The church building covered all of the purchased land except for about a foot around the perimeter. Father Linahan got permission from Southern Pacific Railroad to extend the buildings and establish a parking lot. Such permission was almost unheard of, but it was granted. Attractive additions have been made in recent years.

Church of the Nazarene

Oakridge Church of the Nazarene was organized by District Superintendent Hess in March of 1950 with thirteen Charter Members: Violet Conner, Fae Conner, David Conner, Mr. and Mrs. Elza Cross, Harold Cross, Alma Cross, Michael Cross, Claude Schmidt, Barbara Schmidt, Gerald Schmidt, Mildred Schmidt and Ronald Schmidt. The first pastor was the Rev. Arlie B. Conner.

With Rev. Conner's arrival, regular Sunday services and mid-week meetings were begun at the home of Claude Schmidt. Soon the building on Main Street was purchased, where the congregation worshipped for several years.

The next move was to its present location on Highway 58, under the leadership of Pastor Leroy Harris. On Easter Sunday, 1955, the congregation moved into its new church, valued at $50,000. Members of the building committee were Jim Hanson, Claude Schmidt and Ellsworth Peterson.

By 1975, a larger church was needed and land for the new building was donated by the Larry Weddle family. Architect Don Eby drew up the plans and groundbreaking took place December 4, 1977. The property value exceeded $700,000 when the project was complete.

The 1978-79 church board was made up of Stewards: Jill Gardner, Violet Hanson, Ann Peterson, Mildred Schmidt and Edna Thompson; and Trustees: Ellsworth Peterson, Harold Cross, Paul Ferrigno and Dave Taylor. Craig Gardner was chairman of Christian Life. Virginia Ellis was NWMS President and David Hubbard was NYI President.

The church was completed in early 1979 and then was dedicated on March 11, 1979. Since that time, the people have completed the two parking lots totalling more than 50,000 square feet of space.

The church reached its peak attendance to date in 1983 when it averaged 195 in the worship service. Since then it has declined to the present 113 average in the worship service. Much of this decline is due to the economic situation of the city from which many families have moved away.

St. Luke Lutheran Church

Lutheran services were first held in 1935 at the old movie and community hall at Westfir, which was located across the street from the Westfir grocery store. Meetings were conducted the third Sunday of each month at three in the afternoon.

Early members included William Tuchardt, Sr., his wife Anna and their children Henry, Charles and Emma; William Tuchardt, Jr., his wife Leah and children; Herbert Tuchardt, his wife Frances and children; the Fredrich Buettner family; Mrs. Vesta Wessner and daughters; Mrs. Cecil Tucker and children; and the Greer family of Oakridge.

The St. Luke congregation was formally organized in 1935 and constructed a church on School Street in 1954. This building burned in 1965. The fire was a spectacular one caused by the explosion of oil tanks on an adjacent lot which engulfed the church.

The congregation purchased property on Teller Road and built the present church which was dedicated in 1967.

In 1973, about half the property purchased in 1965 was sold to Peterson Builders. This property now contains the Ironwood Village Apartments.

In 1984, a committee to make plans for a sunday school addition was formed. Committee members were: Keith Murry, Sharon Wick, Shirleen Perigny, Hans Dappert, John Bascom and Pastor Tim VanNatta.

When the plans were final, Bill Gilbert was chosen as the general contractor and cost was minimized by a great deal of congregational involvement in the building. Del Darby agreed to lead the work force with Jake David, Al Hickman, Jim Paddock and Pastor VanNatta serving as his right-hand men along with many other members of the congregation who worked when schedules allowed.

The work started July 12, 1987, and the new building — consisting of 1,920 square feet with three classrooms, restrooms, supply room, church office and pastor's study — was dedicated on December 6, 1987.

The Church of Jesus Christ of Latter-Day Saints

The members of the Church of Jesus Christ of Latter-Day Saints started meeting in Oakridge in 1947 in the home of Gilbert and Mertel Nelson. In the early 1950's, Andy Draper was Presiding Elder and they met at the Oddfellows Hall.

The Church of Jesus Christ of Latter-Day Saints, built in the 1980's on McFarland Road, Oakridge, Oregon.

Over the years before the church was built on McFarland Road, the members met in a number of places such as the Seventh-Day Adventist Church, Westfir Community Church, Westfir School gymnasium, Union Hall, Greenwaters Park and in a vacant building next to Town Tavern. They also met at homes of members when a building was not available.

Some of the men who have served as branch president are: Ivan P. Ballard, Leland Montgomery, Boyde Bowles, Lloyd Jackson, Arthur Scroggins, Gary Washburn, Richard Stephens, Grant Elkington and Bruce Barnes.

The LDS Church has been built on their five acres. The original chapel has 2,000 square feet of space and the addition, valued at $750,000, has 6,000 square feet of space. There is seating capacity of 186 in the chapel and with attached cultural hall will seat 275. The cultural hall will seat 110 for dinner and also serve as a half-court basketball court for youth.

The LDS Church is a handsome building located near the Circle Bar Golf Club.

Oakridge Methodist Church

The first known historical material concerning Oakridge Methodist Church was compiled by Claude Jones. Some of it appeared in a newspaper article on July 14, 1959 (name of paper unknown). Part of it is as follows:

"The earliest church services I could find any record of were taken from a diary kept by Georgie Singletary. First mention of church services was January 17, 1915. She attended July 22, November 11, 1917, and January 18 and August 25, 1918 — so you can readily see about how regularly and how often church services were held."

The first official board was composed of Charlie Paddock, J.D. Ash and Claude Jones.

To give impetus to the church project, Paddock and his wife donated the land for a building site, and Paddock and Jones arranged necessary financing for materials.

About this time, a young man named Clarence Currier came to Oakridge from Sutherlin, Oregon, and, in 1925, with the volunteer help of his two brothers and some congregation members, he built the church. "Neither he nor his brothers received any compensation for their work," Jones reported, it being a freewill offering.

In 1959, the old church was torn down to make way for a spacious, new one. Lloyd Howard and Walt Kissinger were directors of construction. Ernest Sittser was chairman of the building committee. Ralph Peinecke took the chairman job when Sittser moved away. Over 33 men worked regularly each week on the construction as volunteers. Eighteen out-of-town men came and helped put on the roof. Thirty pickup loads of rock were brought from the hills for the south wall. Earl Walker constructed the cross for the exterior of the church.

The first service was held in the new church on December 11, 1960.

Kingdom Hall of Jehovah's Witnesses

The Kingdom Hall on Maple Street in Oakridge was built in 1954 by members of the local congregation. The building has been improved several times. The last renovation was done in 1986.

The history of Jehovah's Witnesses in Oakridge goes back to 1888, when a pioneer settler from Kansas moved his family to High Prairie where several members acquired homesteads.

A congregation was formed in 1925 and meetings were held in private homes. The house next to the fire hall had a sign on the front, identifying it as the Kingdom Hall. In the 1920's, special meetings were held in the local theatre, on the north side of Hazel Street.

In the 1890's, Jehovah Witnesses were known as "International Bible Students." The designation "Kingdom Hall" for places of worship was first used by Jehovah's Witnesses in 1935 in Hawaii.

CHAPTER XIV

Waldo Lake Irrigation and Power Company

In May of 1905, Amos Black laid claim to 100,000 acre feet of water in Waldo Lake and reserved the right to store an additional 150,000 acre feet of water.

It took a trip to Washington, D.C., and 26 months of negotiation with the Forest Service to get the permit to dig a channel to drain water from the lake.

There were to be three major players in the scheme: Amos Black, for whom Black Creek is named; Frederick Ray, a promoter to whom Black sold most of his water rights and for whom the 7,000-foot Mt. Ray is named; and Simon Klovdahl, the civil engineer from Eugene who built the headgate, a 28 by 40 foot concrete dam-like structure at Klovdahl Bay, which bears his name.

The investors figured to make money by selling irrigation rights, by developing land for irrigation and selling it and by producing power.

Waldo Lake has no permanent inlet, but they figured the lake would refill each winter from snow melt. However, a 1964 study estimated it would take 10 years for the lake to refill if it were drained 40 feet.

Klovdahl began work in 1909. His crew built trails to the work site and a 5-mile wagon road from the north end of Waldo Lake to connect with a wagon road that led east to Shaniko, then the nearest rail point.

The channel idea was abandoned. The headgate and tunnel through rock behind the headgate would be used. The tunneling began in 1910. They used drills and dynamite to blast through 500 feet of rock. Their tools and materials were shipped to Shaniko from Portland, hauled to the lake by wagon and ferried across the lake by boat. Part of the supplies were brought in on horseback from Oakridge.

Money was short and the work was hard. The season was also short. Frederick Ray raised less than half the $125,000 he originally estimated the project would cost. He died in 1914. Klovdahl had complained about the lack of money to meet payroll and buy supplies. He accepted stock in the company in lieu of his own salary. He quit in 1914 just before they would have completed the system.

The company held together another 20 years under different management. In 1927, they rehired Klovdahl to make repairs in the headgate. They were aware of a major leak.

In 1934, two years after Klovdahl died, the Forest Service terminated the company's special-use permit and the area reverted to Forest Service jurisdiction.

In the spring of 1987, it was reported that 300 gallons of water per minute were leaking from the tunnel.

Dave Nordenson, Paul Claeyssens and other Forest Service people were in the old tunnel in July of 1987. They took pictures and inspected the tunnel before having it sealed with concrete brought in by helicopter.

Paul Claeyssens is a cultural resource specialist for the Forest Service. He has determined that the structure is eligible for placement on the National Register of Historic Places. In his 21-page report on Klovdahl "Dam" he sums up the report this way:

"Today the headgate and tunnel remain a tribute to the engineers and workers who struggled so hard to make the dreams of a few water-power speculators come true, and it is a tangible reminder that the beautiful Waldo Lake area as we know it today could have been rendered a highly modified ecosystem if the unfolding of history had taken a slightly different course."

Today the dam and headgates can be seen from Klovdahl Bay. Topping the headgate are eight cogwheel valves, which were built to raise and lower the bronze water gates. When the gates were raised, water would have flowed through the tunnel and into Black Creek.

CHAPTER XV
City of the Upper Willamette

Robert Straub has called it, "that jewel of a city, in the mountains," but the trading hub of the Upper Willamette has had many names. When white men first came to the area they called it Big Prairie and later, because the voting precinct and the post office were named Hazeldell, Big Prairie became Hazeldell. In 1912, the name was changed to Oakridge.

The city is located above the fog line and below the snow line. It is so ideally located that when Ruby Lund was writing a column for the *Oakridge Telegram*, she called the city the Shangrila of the Cascades.

Banking services came to Oakridge in November of 1947 when the First National Bank of Oregon sent Vernon "Cap" Ricks to town to establish a bank. He opened a bank in temporary quarters at the old Ed Clark garage building, now the Town Tavern. Banking service was carried on there until the present bank building was complete.

The Chamber of Commerce and the Lions Club started here in 1948.

In 1948, the city hall was a small frame building, not at all like the present handsome city hall that houses the city offices and a library.

A city fire department was organized in 1947 when Lorenz Gerspach was mayor, and the first fire chief was Dale Ensminger.

From 1860 to 1910, there were mostly homesteaders and trappers in the area so there were not many businesses. When the railroad came, it changed all that. The trainmen needed hotels and restaurants, so the town began to grow. Still, it did not grow as fast as Westfir.

In the 1930's and 40's, Westfir had the medical facilities, theatre and stores. It was a company town. It had a community hall and a place for kids to swim.

An old Oregon State 1937 highway map shows only a gravel road from Oakridge to the Willamette Summit. There was no winter travel and only the adventuresome traveled in the summer. The railroad was the way to go.

The City of Oakridge was incorporated in 1934. Before incorporation of the city, the water supply came from a small spring, and cesspools were the sum total of the sewer system. Privies lined the alley of the main street.

Incorporation grew out of a need for a clean and dependable supply of water and a sewage system. Of the business people on the main street, Charlie and Jim Paddock were in favor of incorporation and Harvey Harkins and Oscar McAtee were opposed. A vote was taken and the City of Oakridge was incorporated in 1934.

Another city grew when McAtee built a new store at the west end of town. The store is now Kentree Market. Willamette City was an unincorporated area until 1966 when it was annexed by request and became a part of Oakridge in order to hook up with the sewer and water supply of Oakridge.

Oakridge's first water system after incorporation came from an intake at Salmon Creek Falls and the primary water line ran down East First Street. It was a redwood water line. Later the city put in deep wells to supply the area.

The first electric plant was a diesel generator owned by Claude Jones. Claude also owned an ice plant and cold storage locker, and he sold ice blocks to the railroad. Mel Minkler was the last owner of the ice plant. The building was torn down in the 1950's. It was located in the parking lot across from the present First Interstate Bank.

Highway 58 was finished in 1940 and that brought more people through the area. It was a help to the town and to the resorts east of town.

The greatest growth for Oakridge came in 1946 with the building of the Pope & Talbot mill and logging operations. (See Logging and Lumber chapter.)

A Masonic Temple was constructed in the 1950's. A new telephone system was built. On September 6, 1954, the Chamber of Commerce held a big party and dance to celebrate the paving of First Street in the business district of Oakridge.

Merton Wilson was a stone mason who built a number of buildings in Oakridge including one at First and Beech where he had a cold storage and locker plant for townspeople.

The city and the schools just got adjusted to the growth of the late 1940's and early 50's when another boom started with the building of Hills Creek Dam. Construction started on the $45 million plus project in 1956. Clearing and preliminary work was done by many contractors. Green and Tecon Construction Company was the prime contractor for over $20 million of the work. Some of the smaller contractors who worked on the project were: P.S. Lord Construction Co., Goulter Construction Co., Goodfellow Bros., Donald Drake Construction and many smaller subcontractors.

The population of Oakridge swelled while construction was going on. The project was completed and a dedication was held on August 4, 1962. It is a flood control dam with hydroelectric capacity. It also created a large recreation area behind it. It is an Army Corps of Engineers project. Phil Cole was one of the engineers and it was through his efforts that Salmon Creek revetment was completed in November of 1959.

In December of 1955, Salmon Creek had flooded causing lots of damage along the eastern part of Oakridge. The damage from that flood made it possible for the City of Oakridge to work with the Corps of Engineers on building the Salmon Creek revetment. The flood of 1964 did a lot of damage to the revetment and much of it had to be rebuilt.

A new $78,000 city hall was built in 1961 and dedicated in January of 1962. Lawrence Hills was Mayor and the council members were: Al Rue, Paul Harmon, Richard Behr, Bud Anderson, Harry Worth and Peter Klosterman. The architects were Stafford-Moran-Longwood and the contractor was A.E. Stafford Construction.

Edith Williams was Oakridge City Recorder for 28 years. She retired in 1974. Other city recorders have been: Fred Dorfler, Dale Helikson, Charles Paddock, Laura Stalcup and Sharon Kutch.

The Mayors have been: Harvey Harkins, 1933; James Paddock, 1934; Eldon Templeman, 1941; Charles Croner, 1944; Lorenz Gerspach, 1947; Lawrence Cook, 1951; Arthur Bayly, late 1951; Eldon Forbis, 1953; Kenneth Randall, 1955; Lawrence Hills, 1959 and 1963; Ronel Paddock, 1971 and 1975; Peter Klosterman, 1967 and 1979;

Arion Redmond, 1983; and Richard Culbertson, 1987.

The city has three city parks: Salmon Creek Park on Hills Street, Osprey Park in West Oakridge and the largest, Greenwaters Park, east of town. In the 1960's there was a swimming pool, a wading pool and a building with showers and dressing rooms. Swimming classes were held there each summer.

When the pool could no longer be repaired, it was filled in with sand and the bathhouse was torn down.

Members of the Oakridge Garden Club have spent many volunteer hours planting and caring for flowers in Greenwaters Park. For many years, Lawrence Hills put in days and days of improving the park.

The Oakridge Airport is on a hill west of the city. It has a paved runway and apron and can handle twin-engine planes.

The Oakridge Pioneer Museum was opened in 1959 at 76243 Pine Street. On display are artifacts that were used by the early settlers and are being preserved for future generations.

Citizens of the Year

It has been the custom every year since 1948 to honor people who have been outstanding in community service. For several years the Lions Club and the Chamber of Commerce sponsored the event. In recent years it has been one of the major events sponsored by the Chamber.

Honors have gone to the following people:

Senior First Citizens — 1948, Bessie "Ma" Miller; 1949, George Cline; 1950, Rose Hopkins; 1951, Eldon Forbes; 1952, Lynn Simpson; 1953, Louise Clark; 1954, Art Cooper; 1955, Lawrence Hills; 1956, Roy Temple; 1957, Eddie Roberts; 1958, Claude Jones; 1959, Bertha Graham; 1960, Inez Rogers; 1961, Bruce Hemm; 1962, Harry Worth; 1963, Harold Cross; 1964, Wibby Skeens; 1965 through 1969, no records available; 1970, Dale Helikson; 1971, Ken Boyce; 1972, Buck and Veryl Jensen; 1973, Lee Woolridge and Rigmore Hebert; 1974, Norman Husser; 1975, Freddie Tullock; 1976, Gyneth Prouty; 1977, Mary K. Helikson; 1978, Edna Temple and Louis "Scoop" Ryker; 1979, Joy Lee; 1980, Carroll Miller; 1981, Bud High; 1982, Ercle Ramey; 1983, Faye Alexander; 1984, Margaret Dooley and Lillian Williams; 1985, Max Gosnell; 1986, Edwin Hadley and Doug Lagenor; 1987, Ron Crandall; 1988, Alice Putnam; 1989, James and Ruth Jones.

Junior First Citizens: 1959, Dr. LaVern Huff; 1960, Ward Sybouts; 1961, Audrey Rockwell; 1962, Rev. Ted Jones; 1963, Jim Hill; 1964, Dr. Carol Johnson; 1965 to 1969, no records; 1970, Dennis DeHarpport; 1971, none; 1972, Jim Dyer; 1973 and 1974, none; 1975, Steve Nimocks; 1976, Jim Gillespie; 1977, Jane Keefer; 1980, Patsy Gilliam; 1981, Virginia Staley; 1982, Jim Burby and Dale Gardner; 1983, Steve Broome; 1984, Beverly McCulley; 1985, Pam DeLong; 1986, Nancy Armstrong; 1987, Leo Robb; 1988, Tim VanNatta; 1989, Lori McMahon.

Future First Citizens: 1970, Kathy Putnam; 1971, none; 1972, Gary Williamson; 1973, none; 1974, Randy Nash; 1975, none; 1976, Chris Barber; 1977, Sheryl Stone; 1978, Diana Jackson; 1979, Robin McFarland; 1980, Helen Jean Helikson; 1981, Bill Martinson; 1982, Jim Young; 1983, Andrea Armstrong; 1984, Kristin Barstad; 1985, Doty Spencer; 1986, Teri Holly; 1987, Ross Snuggerud; 1988, Kristie Nelson; 1989, Julie Preschun.

CHAPTER XVI
Medical and Legal Services

After Western Lumber Co. built the logging railroad, camps and a sawmill at Westfir, the town became the medical center for the Upper Willamette area.

A series of doctors attended the sick and injured at Westfir Clinic. The doctors were recruited by Max Wright, general manager of the Pacific Hospital Assn. in Eugene, as part of PHA's pre-paid medical plan contract with the lumber company.

A Dr. Dobbins was in Westfir about 1925; and by 1932, Dr. Joseph Benson was in practice there. He lived in a house downstream from the mill office. He lost his wife and child when his house burned.

Dr. George Varney and Dr. Wesley Haffner are best remembered of the early group of doctors. Freddie Tullock, R.N., worked with Dr. Varney from 1939 to 1942. Dr. Haffner stayed in Westfir during World War Two. He left in 1946 so he could raise his family in a larger town.

Dr. Waldo Harris came to take Haffner's place. Harris took over recruiting work that Wright used to do.

When Pope & Talbot came to Oakridge, the community boomed from a railroad village to a growing milltown.

Harris hired other doctors to help him, and he built a clinic at Oakridge when the center of population shifted there.

Dr. Marshall Poole came in 1950 and stayed for 20 years. All of Harris' associates had contracts that prevented them from opening competitive practices of their own. Without any investments in the community, it was easy for them to move elsewhere.

Like many of his associates, Harris, too, left Oakridge in 1959 to become a renowned heart specialist in Eugene. He and University of Oregon track coach Bill Bowerman popularized jogging as a preventative for fatal heart attacks.

Some attempts were made over the years to establish a hospital in Oakridge. A proposal for a tax-supported hospital was voted down. Fund-raising programs also failed.

Dr. Charles Holland and Dr. Louis Bianchini were partners in the clinic in the early 1960's. Other doctors who worked in the clinic in the 50's and 60's were Neil E. Diess, Dale Hunsaker, Joseph Downes, Emmit Woodward, Jacoby, DeWitt, Tyler and Holst.

Frank Tyler had a pharmacy at the clinic. Tommy Thomas was laboratory and X-ray technician. Jeannie Thomas was office manager from 1957 to 1973.

Bobbie McMahon was office manager while the clinic at Oakridge was being built and Westfir clinic was being phased out. In 1949, she worked mornings at Westfir and carried the books to Oakridge to work afternoons. After the move was completed, she worked at Oakridge Clinic until 1955.

In the early 50's, the cost of prenatal care, delivery of a baby and the six-week checkup cost $120. A lot of babies were born at both the Westfir Clinic and at Oakridge Clinic.

Dr. Hughes Brown bought the Oakridge Clinic in 1967. Dr. Poole stayed on until about 1970. Dr. Brown did not have any luck trying to recruit doctors to work in Oakridge so he sold the clinic. He could not keep up with the workload by himself.

Dr. Warren Griffith has a general medical practice at Green Mountain Clinic in the former Oakridge Clinic building.

There is another medical facility on Highway 58. It is the Oakridge Medical Clinic for family and emergency medicine.

In a telephone conversation with Dr. Varney's widow, she said they came to Westfir in 1937 and stayed until 1942 when her husband went the into service. She said her husband never had days off and that he had to go in the service to get a rest. He worked alone at the Westfir Clinic and came to Oakridge in the afternoon for two hours to care for the railroad people. There was an office in the Croner Drug Store. There were lots of railroad people here then. After he was out of the service when the war was over, he went into practice in Springfield and was on the staff of McKenzie-Willamette Hospital. Mrs. Varney has been a McKenzie-Willamette Auxiliary volunteer for 40 years.

Some of the nurses who worked at Oakridge Clinic were: Jane Brieske, Trudy Ridenour, Thelma Humphrey and Josephine Ray.

Dentists who were remembered were Dr. Angelos and Dr. Aiken. Dr. Carol Johnson has had a dental practice in Oakridge for many years and is still in practice. Dr. David Anderson also has a dental practice in Oakridge.

Some of the optometrists who have had offices in Oakridge are Larry Burr, Carol Marusich, Laverne Huff and William A. Dunn.

The Justice Court for the State of Oregon, Upper Willamette District, has had well qualified people serve as Justice of the Peace. They include Fred Dorfler, Georges Bouhey, Raymond Sassaman, Jack Wilkinson, Patti A. Bolin and Robert Peterson.

Only a few attorneys have come to live in the area. Kenneth Randall was a practicing attorney with an office in the building directly across from City Hall. He and his wife had an apartment in the same building.

Some other attorneys who had worked in Oakridge are: Ben Sanchez and Jeffery Lake of Flynn, Lake and Brown. Members of the Bradley and Hawes law firm were also here for a time.

Dale Helikson, long-time City Attorney, had his law office at 48271 East First Street (see *Biographical Sketches, Dale Helikson*). When he retired, he sold his law practice to Richard L. Fredricks.

CHAPTER XVII
The Fish Hatcheries

Fish culture is nothing new to the Upper Willamette. The State of Oregon had hatcheries around the state in the early 1900's.

A trout hatchery was established in Oakridge in 1922. The pond system was a series of earthen ponds, possibly gravel lined, with earth abutments for screen and dam boards. In the 1950's to 1956, the existing hatchery was improved to its present condition. It includes ten 20'x100'x6' raceways, two brood ponds and four circular ponds, all concrete. The buildings include three resident houses, hatchery incubator buildings, garage, office and storage facilities.

The salmon hatchery was established in 1911 and was operated solely as an egg taking and eyeing station during the period of 1911 to 1919. During this period, all eggs were shipped to other hatcheries, principally Bonneville and Kalaskanine. In 1919, the first hatchery facilities were constructed. Charlie Hills was a Salmon Hatchery superintendent for many years.

In the late 1940's, the U.S. Corps of Engineers completely rebuilt Willamette Salmon Hatchery to compensate for the loss of salmon spawning and rearing areas in the Middle Fork of the Willamette River which resulted from construction of Lookout Point Dam. The hatchery construction was completed in 1952.

Dexter holding ponds were immediately constructed below Dexter Dam to provide a collection and holding facility for adult spring Chinook salmon. These ponds were completed and placed in operation in 1955.

The salmon hatchery is operated under contract with the Corps of Engineers. The Corps provides funds for most of the operating expenses and the state pays a portion based on operating expenses incurred during certain years before the hatchery was remodeled.

In the fall of 1983, Willamette Trout Hatchery and the Oakridge Salmon Hatchery were merged into a single operating facility under one manager. The complex is now called Willamette Fish Hatchery. Salmon production is still funded by the Corps of Engineers and trout production is state funded.

Through the years, many millions of trout and salmon have started their lives at these hatcheries, to be released in lakes and streams. Salmon fingerlings are released below Dexter Dam.

It was difficult to find names of managers or superintendents of the hatcheries from years back. Quentin Smith, who was manager from 1973 to 1981, has done his best to furnish some names. Another Mr. Smith was an early-day manager, Archie Anderson was a manager for several years, then Charlie Hansen, Max Frame was manager from 1961 to 1966, and Jim Ray from 1966 to 1973.

The hatcheries were combined in 1983. Trent Stichell was manager and then Tom Herbst, who is current manager.

The many visitors to the hatcheries are surprised to see how many fish are raised to perpetuate the great sport of fishing.

CHAPTER XVIII
Newspapers

The first Oakridge newspaper was published in 1924 by a former Eugene Daily News owner. The local paper was called the Tribune. It did not last long. The next paper was the Oak-Fir Lookout published by Mr. Korstad in 1939 through 1941.

OAK-FIR LOOKOUT
The Only Paper Devoted Exclusively To The Interests of the Upper Willamette Region

FRIDAY, AUGUST 22, 1941

Volume 20 — Number 15   Thursday, January 12, 1967   Price 10c

DEAD MOUNTAIN ECHO
Wednesday, August 9, 1989

Serving the Upper Willamette Valley

Illustrations of Oak-Fir Lookout, Oakridge Telegram and Dead Mountain Echo

In 1947, G.G. (Gerry) Sittser came to Oakridge and published the Oakridge Telegram. Gerry Sittser died in June of 1973.

The Dead Mountain Echo started publication in April of 1973 under the ownership of Dennis Keffer, Mark Schwebke and Frank Drake. It was purchased by Larry Roberts and Dennis Keffer, then later Roberts bought out Keffer. The weekly paper is still published by Roberts as of 1989.

Gerry Sittser, publisher of the Oakridge Telegram for 26 years, was born at Valley Fort, Washington, on February 11, 1911. He was the oldest of 13 children. When he was young, he was involved in many different vocations. He worked with his father on the Willamina News. He later worked on a paper in Delake, Oregon.

He and Esther Beach were married in McMinnville, Oregon, on December 2, 1938. They had four children — Adrain D., Rodney E., Kathleen G. and Laura Lee.

Before his coming to Oakridge, he was involved in the Nelscott News, Oakland Tribune and North Lincoln County News. The first year or so he printed the Oakridge Telegram at the coast, bussing them to Oakridge. Werner Klosterman, a taxi driver, sold ads and delivered the papers. Iola Davis sold subscriptions.

The first Oakridge location of the newspaper was next to Cooper's Craft Shop in Willamette City. The next move was to a new building uptown at the corner of Pine and Commercial, now used as a museum. Bud Long used part of the building for Oakridge Westfir Truck Line freight storage. The next move was to the old Kocer Furniture Store building west of City Hall.

Gerry was a good small town newspaper man. He was good at snooping out the news, but his ideas on matters didn't always jibe with the public. He remarked about the first tree planting, that it would never get off the ground. But it did! When the City of Oakridge was planning a bond issue for a new City Hall he was asked why nothing had been in the paper favoring the issue. He said he was not for it. The next day after going to the hearing and presentation he came out with two columns telling people why they should vote for the bond issue, stating that he had never seens such a good presentation.

Gerry felt a small town paper was necessary to keep the public informed on local issues, even when it was a hard job to do.

As a tribute to Gerry Sittser, clippings from the old Oakridge Telegrams are on swing boards at the Museum, close by to where many of them were printed. Bundles of the old issues are in storage at the museum. We are fortunate to have 26 years of Oakridge history so available.

CHAPTER XIX
Memories

Many people arrived in Westfir during the Depression and worked a few days a week at the mill for $1.80 per day. They had a spirit of community, with Boy Scouts, Girl Scouts, Community Club, Christmas parties, movies and a unique swimming pool. The mill donated the lumber and the men built a slatted pool in the river. The pool had a wooden deck and a diving board. The water could flow through the pool.

A Red Cross swimming instructor came each summer to teach swimming. Everyone in town could use the pool. It was located upriver from the S.P. railroad bridge.

Westfir had a grade school and a high school at one time but now they are part of the Oakridge District and their high school building is now used as a middle school.

Fire protection that was once furnished by the mill now has to be the responsibility of the homeowners.

Where there was once parties, dances, children playing and the sounds of the mill whistle and workmen calling out to each other, there is now only the sound of the river flowing and sometimes a train whistle at the crossing.

A man named John Cain had a homestead downriver from where the Forest Service nursery is at Westfir. He ran a ferry for people who needed to cross the river.

Gladys Lavoy, the daughter of Charles Hebert, remembers it like this. "We never had much money, but our neighbors didn't either, so we made our own fun. We would all get together at someone's home, roll up the rug, get out the fiddle and have a dance. My dad played the fiddle. Sometimes there was someone with a guitar or banjo. We also had quilting bees, taffy pulls, card parties, sleigh rides and sledding parties. The grown-ups and kids all took part."

Jennie Hebert had a laundry in her home on Commercial Street when the railroad was being built on over the hill. Her husband was working building forms for some of the tunnels up the mountain and getting lots of wood when he was home to heat water and dry clothes. There were lines of clothes strung all over the house when the weather was bad, and the wood heater was kept going full blast to dry the laundry. Jennie was also a midwife to many families. Often she was called out in the middle of the night. She would light a lantern and walk sometimes a mile or more to get to the mother who needed her help.

Lois Croner Diess wrote that she and her sister Barbara used to sit on the table in their kitchen and watch out of the window as some pretty interesting fights took place in front of the saloon on Main Street in the early 1930's. It was a lot like the Western movies we see today.

She also remembered walking over the railroad tracks, through the woods across the highway and through more woods to get to the old swimming hole at Greenwaters Park. There was no lifeguard, but she doesn't think there was ever a fatality there in those days.

The 4th of July parades were something to look forward to all year long, decorating the wagons, bicycles and tricycles. All of that ended with World War Two.

There was a telephone switchboard in Croner's Drug Store. When a call came in from someone's relative in the armed forces, Lois would quickly jump on her bike and go tell them a call was waiting. That was a happy time for all.

Another memorable day was when they paved the main street. No more mud to wade through to cross the street.

Lois was born in 1927, so her girlhood memories are in the 1930's and early 1940's, before the war.

Many remember swimming at Greenwaters when it was necessary to hike through the woods to get there (before Highway 58).

Kids in the area pulled sections of the wooden sidewalks into the middle of First Street and pushed over outside privies on Halloween. Once a man was in a privy that got pushed over. His yells for help put fear in the pranksters.

Then there was the year the North Fork froze over. Just once in 60 years! That was the year they could ice skate on the Westfir mill pond.

Families and friends would drive to McCredie Springs to swim and picnic on Sunday afternoons in the summertime.

There were summer baseball games where the fans came in their touring cars and brought their lunches or picnics.

Tamaris Clifford recalls when her father Luther Rogers had a logging camp at Brock Canyon where she spent summers as a child. She said, "The road to Erma Belle Lakes looked like a river bottom. We used to walk to the Brock Canyon meadow where there was a log cabin and a whole field of daisies and Indian paintbrush. We found dinosaur tracks in the rocks and trapped crawdads in the icy creeks. We had a crank-style Forest Service telephone, a wood stove, a bunkhouse, cookhouse and outhouse with pictures and stories all over the walls.

High Prairie Grange

The High Prairie Grange #943 was formed in March of 1962. They were active until they consolidated with Lowell Grange. John Mills, Bill DuMont and Al and Betty Clifford all served as Masters of the Grange.

The Grange was instrumental in getting the Bloodmobile to come to Oakridge. The ladies served refreshments to those who gave blood. The Moose Lodge took over that work when the Grange disbanded.

The Grange contributed money and labor towards the tennis court and softball field at Greenwaters Park. They also gave $200 to help build the entry to the park.

They put on plays that were free to the public. They also had a farm-oriented exhibit at the Lane County Fair each year. They had holiday bazaars with the money going to different local charities.

The Lions Club donated the cedar poles to light the high school football field in 1949. Bert Davis logged the poles and George Thatcher trucked them to the field. Larry Hendrickson, Dick Behr, Harry Clark, Dan Hendrickson and others were involved in the project.

CHAPTER XX

Storms

A big snowstorm in 1937 buried old Camp 3. The county sent two caterpillars with dozers to clear the road so food and supplies could be delivered. Camp 3 was one of six camps owned by Western Lumber Company.

There was another big snowstorm in February of 1949 with many people snowbound for a short time.

In November of 1953, a flood of water came down Eagle Creek washing out a portion of Highway 58 and the Eagle Creek Bridge east of Oakridge.

In December of 1955, Salmon Creek flooded doing much damage along the eastern part of the city. The damage from this flood made it possible for the City of Oakridge to work with the Corps of Engineers for the building of the Salmon Creek revetment. Later flooding did much damage to the revetment.

The flood of 1964 was considered a once-in-a-hundred-years flood. It did terrific damage. Approximately 22 inches of rain and snow fell on top of three feet of wet snow. Water gushed from everywhere. All the streams in the area overflowed taking roadways, timber, bridges and anything in the way downstream with the flood waters. Salt Creek alone did terrific damage, destroying 21 miles of Highway 58 including all bridges. It took out railroad trestles and bridges and caused many slides.

During this storm, Oakridge was isolated for five days. Deception Creek Bridge west of town was washed out. Five Greyhound busses were caught in Oakridge. The passengers were put up at the school until a special train was sent from Eugene and they were taken down to the valley.

It was many months before all the streams, roads and bridges were cleaned up and rebuilt. Highway passage to the summit was closed to traffic because of the great destruction to the roadbed and bridges.

The Hills Creek Dam saved the Willamette City area from severe damage from the 1964 flood.

During the flooding, many men worked filling sandbags to help hold the revetment along Salmon Creek. It was touch and go much of the time, but hard work under hard conditions paid off.

The Columbus Day Storm was the most damaging windstorm in the history of the Northwest. It came on October 12, 1962. Twenty-four lives were lost in Oregon and $170,000,000 in damages. The windstorm cut a swathe through Northern California, Oregon and Washington.

The Oakridge area was not hurt, but timber fell on the summit causing a lot of loss and damage. There were a lot of power outages and road closures. Lane County schools had damages that ran over $289,000. Barometric low point reached 28.41, and winds in the valley were 125 miles per hour with winds at Hebo on the coast reaching 170 miles per hour.

There have been other windstorms that put down timber in the Upper Willamette area, at times closing Highway 58 and other roads until the trees could be removed. These storms usually occur in the fall.

CHAPTER XXI
Geographical Names

ABERNATHY is a railroad station west of Cascade Summit and was named in honor of Governor Abernathy.

BABY ROCK is above the Southern Pacific tracks about five miles southeast of Oakridge and was named by Indians who refused to go near it. They claimed that Indians had died from the bite of animals that inhabited the rock — animals that left tracks resembling the prints of baby feet. The white settlers believed the tracks were made by porcupine.

BRISTOW PRAIRIE was named for Elijah Bristow, the founder of Pleasant Hill, an Oregon pioneer of 1846. Bristow hunted on the prairie and his family grazed cattle there. This prairie straddles the Lane and Douglas County line at the summit of the Calapooya Mountains.

BOX CANYON and BOX CANYON GUARD STATION were named by Charles McClane and Major Sears in 1880. The name is descriptive of the location. A road up the North Fork and through Box Canyon links the Upper Willamette area with the Upper McKenzie area.

BUCK CREEK was named by Fred Warner, a pioneer of 1853 who hunted many seasons at the Buck Creek Camp and killed fine bucks there.

CALAPOOYA MOUNTAINS in southwest Lane County are named for a tribe of Indians who sometimes lived in the Upper Willamette area. A creek in Douglas County is also named for the tribe.

CAMPERS FLAT got its name from its use as the campsite of pioneers who stopped to graze stock at Big Pine Openings.

CHETLE LAKE is northwest of Waldo Lake and is oyster shaped. Chetle is the Chinook word for oyster.

CHRISTY CREEK is a tributary of the North Fork of the Middle Fork of the Willamette River and was named for W. Christy of Eugene who prospected near the creek.

COFFEE POT CREEK received its designation because a pioneer dropped the coffee pot from his wagon here and ran over it with a wagon wheel. The ruined coffee pot was left near this creek.

COWHORN MOUNTAIN is located near the headwaters of the Middle Fork of the Willamette River, has an elevation of 7,664 feet and at one time was called Little Cowhorn, while Mt. Thielsen was called Big Cowhorn. According to the late C.B. McFarland, Little Cowhorn's pinnacle fell off in 1911; and although the mountain is still called Cowhorn, it no longer resembles one.

CRUZATTE was a railroad station near the Cascade summit and was named for Peter Cruzatte, a member of the Lewis and Clark party. When the railroad was being built over the pass, a school was held in a boxcar at this station.

CUPIT MARY MOUNTAIN is named for an Indian woman. Cupit Mary was the last daughter of "Old Moses," an Indian who lived in the vicinity of Oakridge above the Dompier place. Cupit was the Indian word for last. It is said that Cupit Mary was known for her wicked ways.

DEAD MOUNTAIN has an elevation of 3,674 feet and is located just northeast of Oakridge and east of High Prairie. Long ago it was known as Green Mountain, but destructive forest fires through the years drastically altered its appearance and its name changed to Dead Mountain. Fire ravaged the mountain in 1883, 1898, 1910 and 1967. The Dead Mountain Fire of 1910 burned 16,700 acres.

DIAMOND PEAK is that prominent white mountain southeast of Oakridge. It was named for John Diamond, a member of a party of road viewers in search of a pass through the Cascades. These road viewers were in the Diamond Peak area in 1852.

DIAMOND VIEW ADDITION is a residential area of Oakridge that offers a view of Diamond Peak.

EDDEELEO LAKES, located north of Waldo Lake near headwaters of the North Fork, were named for Ed Clark, Dee Wright and Leo McMahon. Ed first saw the lakes in 1912. He and his brother Bert Clark visited the lakes in 1927 and the lakes were stocked with fish in 1929. Clark, Wright and McMahon took cans of fish in by pack horses to stock the lakes. Kelly Sullivan furnished the pack horses and packers. Ed Clark got the fish from a hatchery on the Oregon coast.

EMIGRANT CREEK is a tributary of the Middle Fork of the Willamette River located southwest of Diamond Peak and was named for emigrants of 1853 who made their way to the main river at this point.

ERMA BELL LAKES, located north of Waldo Lake, are named for Miss Erma Bell who was an employee of the United States Forest Service in the Portland office. Erma Bell died in 1918 as a result of an auto accident.

FIELDS, located east of Oakridge, is a station on the railroad named for Joseph and Reuben Fields who were members of the Lewis and Clark expedition.

FISHER CREEK, a tributary of the North Fork located north of Waldo Lake, was named for a pioneer cattleman.

FLAT CREEK, a tributary of Salmon Creek, took its name from the flat area it flows through. There was at one time a ranger station on the flat and the land has a long history of ownership since Squire Hamilton settled there in 1871. Next, Amos Hyland took the place on a debt and sold it to his son-in-law, Al McFarland, who sold it to Almonza McClane. Then McClane sold to a man named Gilbert who was acting for a company that was acquiring land to trade with the government for timber land. The ranger station site was originally selected by Forest Supervisor Clyde Sietz and James Furnish in 1910.

FURNISH CREEK is a tributary to Salmon Creek and was named for James Furnish, a forest ranger who had stated that there was no north fork to Salmon Creek. Therefore, when it was discovered, it was named for him.

GOLD LAKE is south of Waldo Lake near Highway 58 and was named for Mr. Gold who was a foreman for a contractor named Black who worked on the Waldo Lake Irrigation and Power Company tunnel.

GRAY CREEK, located just west of Oakridge, was named for pioneer rancher Israel J. Gray who took a homestead at Gray Creek.

HECKLETOOTH MOUNTAIN, east of Oakridge, was named by Elizabeth Stewart Warner (Mrs. Fred Warner) in 1870. The tall rocks at the summit reminded her of the teeth of a heckle, a tool used for handling flax. Mr. and Mrs. Warner were members of the "Lost Wagon Train" of 1853.

HILLS CREEK flows into the Middle Fork of the Willamette River at Jasper and bears the name of Cornelius Hills, a pioneer of 1847 who crossed the Plains three times. (See George Riddle's *Early Days in Oregon* and Walling's *History of Lane County*.)

HILL'S CREEK, located south of Oakridge, is a tributary of the Middle Fork of the Willamette River and was named for pioneer John H. Hill who had a wife named Phoebe. They settled at the mouth of Hill's Creek in 1870. There was a post office at the ranch from June of 1882 to December of 1885 with John Hill as postmaster. The post office was called Hill.

HUCKLEBERRY CREEK, a tributary of the North Fork of the Middle Fork of the Willamette River, got its name from the abundance of huckleberries in the area.

HUCKLEBERRY FLAT is near Huckleberry Creek and was the location of an old railroad logging camp about 1925 to 1935. The camp was operated by the sawmill at Westfir.

JASPER is a community southeast of Springfield named for the first son of Sophronia and Cornelius Hills. The child was born in Jasper in 1859 and the community was named about 1880.

KELSEY CREEK, east of Oakridge, is a tributary of Salmon Creek and was named for a pioneer family.

KITSON SPRINGS, located on Hill's Creek south of Oakridge, was operated as a resort for many years. The springs and a ridge north of them are named for Dave Kitson, founder of the resort.

KLOVDAHL BAY on Waldo Lake is named for Simon Klovdahl who was an engineer associated with the Waldo Irrigation and Power Company.

KOTCH MOUNTAIN west of Waldo Lake was named for Trapper Louie Kotch who lived in a cabin at the base of this mountain. He was last seen at Hazeldell in 1912. He is believed to have perished in the mountains. His body was never found although the remains of his dog were discovered.

LOWELL CREEK, a tributary of Christy Creek northeast of Oakridge, was named for E.D. Lowell, a pioneer stockman who grazed his stock at the head of Lowell Creek.

LARISON CREEK, a tributary of the Middle Fork of the Willamette River south of Oakridge, was named for George Larison, a pioneer logger.

McCREDIE SPRINGS, located ten miles southeast of Oakridge on Salt Creek, were named for W.W. McCredie who bought an interest in the springs about 1916. Before then, the springs were known as Winino Springs.

MIDDLE FORK OF THE WILLAMETTE RIVER is the main tributary of the Willamette River and heads in Lake Timanogas high in the Cascades near the Douglas County line.

MOOLACK MOUNTAIN is north of Waldo Lake, has an elevation of 5,500 feet and gets its name from the word "elk," which in Chinook is Moolack.

PACKARD CREEK, a tributary of the Middle Fork of the Willamette River, is located south of Oakridge and was named for a pioneer logger of the 1870's.

PENGRA was a station on the Southern Pacific line located northwest of Lowell.

It was named for Bynon J. Pengra (see Pengra Pass).

PENGRA PASS, located west of Odell Lake, was also named in honor of Bynon J. Pengra who found the pass in 1865 when he and W.H. Odell were on a trip to inspect the work on the Oregon Central Military Road. Pengra was in charge of construction of the Military Road.

PIONEER GULCH is southeast of Oakridge on the Middle Fork of the Willamette River and was named in honor of the pioneers of 1853 whose wagon tracks are still visible. The first wagon train over the Willamette Pass reached the river near this gulch. The marker that now stands in Greenwaters Park commemorating these pioneers was first placed at Pioneer Gulch and later moved to the park where it could be viewed by more people than might make the trip to Pioneer Gulch.

PADDY VALLEY is near Timpanogas Lake and got its name from the many beaver in the area. Early trappers called beavers "paddies" because of their flat tails.

RATTLESNAKE BUTTE is west of Dexter and was named by Elijah Bristow because of the great number of rattlesnakes found near the butte. Bristow was a pioneer of 1846.

SALT CREEK is a large tributary of the Middle Fork of the Willamette River and got its name from the salt springs along its banks.

SALT CREEK FALLS were discovered and named by Frank Warner and Charlie Tufti in 1887. The falls are near Willamette Pass Ski Area just off Highway 58.

SALT CREEK HIGHWAY TUNNEL, built in 1939 by Kuckenberg Construction Company, was named for nearby Salt Creek. Earl Clark of Oakridge, who worked on the tunnel, said that the rock taken from the blue rock formation was chiseled by hand by stone workers from Italy.

STALEY CREEK, a tributary of the Middle Fork of the Willamette River south of Oakridge and just north of the Calapooya range, is named for W.F. Staley who was a U.S. Forest Service employee. This creek was known for a time as the South Fork of the Middle Fork of the Willamette River.

STALEY RIDGE runs parallel to Staley Creek and was named for W.F. Staley.

SKOOKUM CREEK, a tributary of the North Fork of the Middle Fork of the Willamette River, was named by Indians who traveled the old Indian trail from Foley Springs on the McKenzie to the Upper Willamette area.

TAYLOR BUTTE is located north of Waldo Lake and has an elevation of 5,825 feet. It was named about 1898 for Joe Taylor who grazed sheep in the area.

TIPTOP was the name of an early post office near Hill's Creek. Isaac Hamner was the postmaster and his nickname was Tiptop. The post office operated from 1895 to 1901. Locality of Tiptop was later called The Boulders and at one time was owned by Cliff Morgan.

TIRE CREEK is located northwest of Oakridge and is a tributary of the Middle Fork of the Willamette River. It got its name when a tire came off a wagon wheel and rolled into the creek. The wagon tire lay in the creek for years. As a result, people called the stream "Tire Creek."

WININO was a post office on Salt Creek in 1924. Vivian Cartwright was postmaster. Winino Springs has had at least three names with changes of ownership. They were first discovered in 1906 by F.A. Warner who, with two other men, filed for a permit for ten acres covering the mineral springs. The three men paid an annual fee of $25 for the permit. They built two small cabins of logs and shakes and continued the fee, hoping to hold out until the railroad came. The springs were first called Salt Creek Springs, then Winino and later McCredie Springs.

ZION was a post office in the Lost Creek area and was given its name because of nearness to Mt. Zion to the east. This post office operated from 1899 to 1913 with Thomas Hunsaker as postmaster.

Old Wolf Homestead on High Prairie, 1908 — Photo courtesy Claude Hebert

CHAPTER XXII
Resorts and Festivals

McCredie Springs Resort

The hot mineral springs were first discovered by Frank A. Warner who, with two other men, filed for a use permit for ten acres covering the springs. They paid an annual fee of $25 for the permit.

McCredie Hot Springs Resort in the 1950's.

They built two small log-and-shake cabins and continued to pay the annual fee hoping to hold out until the railroad came. They named the springs Salt Creek Springs.

The railroad did come as far as Oakridge by 1912. The road bed or grade was built a few miles east of Oakridge but rails were not put down. This grade was used as a road to the springs for a number of years.

John Hardin of Portland came to the area in 1914 and tried to file a mineral claim on 40 acres that included the springs, but failed. He then leased the site and built a lodge 54x120 feet. To do so, he first built a small sawmill and cut lumber on the site from nearby timber.

He built the lodge but was short of funds for improvements and working capital. He encouraged John and Margaret Cartwright of Harrisburg to become his partners. They repaired and improved the lodge and operated it. The springs were called Winino Springs for a time but by 1926 they were called McCredie Springs. Vivian Cartwright was listed as postmaster of Winino in 1924 and as postmaster of McCredie Springs in 1926.

W.W. McCredie, for whom the springs were renamed, bought an interest in the resort and added cabins and other improvements. The main lodge had 18 rooms, a restaurant and a lounge. Separate from the main lodge, at the west end of the compound and nearer to the highway, there was a service station and small grocery store.

The resort flourished after the highway was completed in 1940, when folks could then come by train or car. In the 1940's and 50's, it was a popular place to go to dine or to stay for a time. Many Oakridge-Westfir organizations frequented the resort for meetings and banquets.

In 1958, the lodge burned to the ground and the flood of 1964 took out all the other facilities. The springs continue to pour forth hot mineral water, and, as of 1989, the leaseholders are seeking investors to build the resort anew.

Willamette Pass Ski Resort

In the late 1930's, ski enthusiasts in Eugene and Springfield wanted a place to ski closer to home. Their first hurdle was selling the U.S. Forest Service on the idea.

Helga Behr at Willamette Pass, December 1947 — Photo courtesy Harry Clark.

In 1939, some Forest Service people and others, including George Korn, Lou Waldorf, Leo Paschelke, Bill McCready, Roy Elliot and Bud Burgess, set out up the as yet unopened Willamette Highway. The purpose of the trip was to find a suitable place on the pass for a ski development.

Seventy miles from Eugene at the 5,000-foot summit, north of Odell Lake and off the highway, they found what they wanted. The area was covered with timber and would not have caught a second look by skiers from Timberline and Baldy's wide open spaces.

In 1941, the Upper Willamette Winter Sports Association was

formed. Prime movers were Dr. Omar Gullion, Dorr Hamlin and George Korn. Brush parties got underway and timber was removed. Roy and Edna Temple of Oakridge were also involved in the clearing process and they were owners of the tow rights for nine years.

While the Temples operated the ski area, it became a significant recreation area with 500 to 1,000 people on a weekend. Edna served hot drinks and chili to the skiers.

Temple sold out to George Korn about 1950. By 1951, the main slope — all man cleared — measured 2,500 feet, served by a rope tow and skiable with six inches of snow. There was a bunny slope, served by rope tow, and a jumping site along with a run for steep slope skiing. There was a snack shack and warming hut with equipment rental service.

Overnight accommodations were at Crescent Lake and McCredie Springs. Ski instructors at that time were Mr. and Mrs. Van Purdy, Phil Edbloom and Sam Winn.

In 1954, Cascade Summit postmaster Florence Adkison worked at the Willamette Pass snack shack on weekends. She would snap on cross-country skis for a two-and-one-half mile run to the ski area to put in a full day tending skiers' orders for hot chocolate, coffee and food. At dusk, she would make her cross-country run back to her Cascade Summit home.

Jack Meissner, who made an impressive 300-mile cross-country journey from Mt. Hood to Crescent Lake in 1948, is the son of Florence Adkison. His wife and children are also ski enthusiasts.

In the years from 1955 to 1985, there were a number of operators at Willamette Pass. Now in 1989 it has four chair lifts and a large lodge with restaurant, lounge and ski shop. It is operated by Willamette Pass Ski Corporation.

Kitson Hot Mineral Springs — Oakridge, Oregon

Dave Kitson obtained claim to the hot mineral springs about 1869. He built a swimming pool of hand-hewn logs; but in 1891; a natural dam above the springs

Kitson Springs Resort in the 1950's. Hills Creek in foreground.

broke and washed the pool away. Kitson also made bathtubs of hewn cedar logs. He made wooden spigots and water was held in the tubs by plugging the drains with eight-inch wooden plugs.

Dave Kitson also built a log house for himself and a rooming house near the spring for guests.

By 1908, Mrs. B.B. Warfield was operating the resort. At that time, people came to the springs by horse and wagon. In 1915, a new hotel or lodge was built and Mrs. Warfield's daughter, Mrs. McAlister, operated the resort. By the 1930's, automobiles could get to the resort; but because of hard times, the resort was sold and the new owners leased it to Bill Cash. He operated it for some time but also found it hard to make a profit.

Finally, Ed Huntington and Don Beckman, who made up the B&H Corporation, were owners of the 160-acre resort property. In 1963, Lane County health authorities condemned the hotel, bathhouse and all, for failure to meet county health codes. Because the cost of bringing the resort up to code was so great, it was never again open to the public.

Sun Deck at Kitson Springs Resort in the 1950's.

The property was given to the Oregon Trail Boy Scout Council. It is used by the Scouts for camping and other activities. Mr. and Mrs. Marvin Bailey were caretakers for the Oregon Trail Scout Council. Clara Bailey also worked with the Boy Scouts in Oakridge.

The caretaker's house is the only building at the resort that is in use. The swimming pool deteriorated and broke up about 1980. There are only a few remnants of the once busy hot springs resort where people came by wagon, train and auto to seek health and relaxation.

The Lake Resorts

The resorts at Crescent Lake and at both the east and west ends of Odell Lake are popular for boating, fishing and camping in summer and for cross-country skiing in winter. They are all accessible from Highway 58.

Tree Planting Festival

Willard Trumbull had an idea.

While growing up in the Portland area, Trumbull developed a firm appreciation for Oregon's pristine environment, especially its vast timberlands. Even though he moved away from Oregon for a short period, Trumbull carried that fondness with him and he returned to live in Oakridge in 1952.

First Tree Planting Site revisited after 35 years. Pictured left to right, John Marconi, Ilena Fleming, Ron Crandall and Bob Obermeyer. Photo taken April, 1988. Thirty-five year old trees in background.

"I missed the trees," Trumbull said from his Eugene home. "People should be glad and fortunate to have those trees. I did. I grew up in Oregon."

Trumbull, who owned and operated a photography shop in Oakridge in 1952, spearheaded efforts to host a tree planting day in the area. Little did he know that his idea would turn out to be the foundation for many tree planting extravaganzas to come.

On April 13, 1953, Trumbull asked the Oakridge Chamber of Commerce to sponsor an annual tree planting day. His wish was granted. Soon his idea gained support and enthusiasm from citizens, Forest Service personnel, businessmen, congressmen, state legislators and radio, television and newspaper reporters.

"Everyone was real supportive. The local newspaper was behind it all the way. The business people were willing to get it started."

Plans to coordinate the community's first annual event took a few weeks to complete. Because of its late start, the planting date was pushed back to late fall. Ranger Bill Cummins of the Oakridge Ranger District was called on to furnish an area in the Willamette National Forest to plant. A 10-acre site (Wall Creek Unit No. 1) along the Salmon Creek drainage was selected for planting on November 14, 1953.

Committees were formed and put to work, and soon the pageant took shape. On Tree Planting Day, a parade formed at Oakridge High School around 10:00 A.M. on a bright, overcast day. The parade marched down First Street through the middle section of town. The big parade included a motorcade, the Boy Scouts, Lane County Mounted Sheriff's posse and other organizations.

After the conclusion of the parade, people drove to the site and began planting trees between string lines. The lines were 15 feet apart and ran from the road to the end of the unit. Businessmen turned out in working clothes with shovels or large trowels in hand. School children from all grades, parents, Boy Scouts and even the dignitaries also assisted in planting an estimated 6,000 seedlings.

Since its beginning, Oakridge-Westfir's annual Tree Planting Festival has grown in stature. Rich in tradition, the event's primary purpose is to replace trees that have been removed by logging, to stimulate interest in conservation and to promote community spirit. Since its inception in 1952, the community has planted thousands of seedlings each year.

From this beginning, the annual festival has grown to a four-day affair. Many activities have been added to attract the young and the old.

The Tree Planting Association Presidents and the Chamber of Commerce and all those who help make the festivals a success put in countless hours of volunteer time. It is a time for the community to think about the environment and to help replace a great resource.

Oakridge works hard for the title "Tree Planting Capital of the World." At a time when so much of the world's forests are being cut and not replaced, it is good to see a place where people care enough about the future to replant what is cut.

Each year a young woman is chosen to rule over the festival and this is the list of those Tree Planting Festival Queens:

1953 Marlene Elam	1966 Janet Demagalski	1978 Julie Anthony
1954 Sharon Racy	1967 Jill Bushong	1979 Suzie Breckel
1955 Mayme Nelson	1968 Nancy Wilcox	1980 no queen
1956 Linda Bigger	1969 Penny Hill	1981 Mikal McPherson
1957-8 Patricia Beard	1970 Wendy Wilcox	1982 Kris Pahle
1959 Michelle Olson	1971 Gale Burgen	1983 Trisha Woods
1960 Pat Welborn	1972 Debbie Thompson	1984 Raquel Farrier
1961 Karen Klosterman	1973 Janet Hansen	1985 Becky Pertuska
1962 Franci Allard	1974 Shawna Lee	1986 Heidie Upmeyer
1963 Kathie Gillispie	1975 Erin Prouty	1987 Libby Hebert
1964 Peggy Rachor	1976 Julie Stout	1988 Shawnna Durand
1965 Paula Buckner	1977 Brenda Lee	1989 Marsha Jones

Judge Waldo Days

Judge Waldo Days is the first weekend in August at Oakridge. The city celebrates with an International Friendship Hike to Mount Fuji to view the "Waldo Country." Hikers gather at the Oakridge Museum on Saturday morning at 9:00 A.M. They are bussed to the hiking area and return in the early afternoon.

There are activities in Greenwaters Park such as art and crafts sales, food concessions, square dancing in the evening and country, folk and bluegrass music all afternoon.

A highlight of the festival is the Waldo Family Reunion and reception at the park on Saturday. There is also a Sunday hike to one of the trees marked by Judge Waldo, bicycle races and a fly fishing exhibition. There is a golf tournament on Sunday.

Judge John B. Waldo

Judge Waldo was an explorer, conservationist, sportsman, scholar and more. He spent many summers in the mountains above Oakridge from 1887 until his death in 1907. This was before there really was a place called Oakridge.

He would leave his home in Salem, travel south, stop at Jasper to visit the Hills family, come up river to Big Prairie and on to the Rigdon's near Summit Lake. Mrs. Rigdon would cook for the party while they rested there, then sell them bread to take on to their camps.

The Judge traveled with a party of three or four men. They made camps, fished, hunted and explored the Cascades.

Waldo Lake, Waldo Glacier, Waldo Mountain, Waldo Wilderness Council and Judge Waldo Days Festival, the first weekend in August at Oakridge, are named for him. The hikes around Waldo Lake and the hike to Fuji Mountain that overlooks Waldo Lake are popular events during Waldo Days.

Judge Waldo's parents came to Oregon in 1843 with the Applegate party. Judge John B. Waldo was born in Marion County on October 8, 1844. He graduated from Willamette University in 1866, was admitted to the state bar in 1870 and married Clara A. Humason in 1877. Their only child was a daughter, Edith. Camp Edith at Waldo Lake was named for her.

The Pioneer Picnic

The first Sunday after the 4th of July each year, the Oakridge Museum sponsors the Pioneer Picnic. Those who have lived in the Westfir-Oakridge area are invited to bring their families, some food and table service, goodwill and memories and get together for a good time.

It is a day of visiting, singing or listening and just having a good time with old friends and new ones.

Descendants of the early pioneers are especially invited. The picnic starts at high noon and the museum opens at one o'clock. Group pictures of the gathering, which are ordered and sold through the museum, are taken just before the picnic. The Pioneer Picnic takes place at Greenwaters Park.

CHAPTER XXIII
Biographical Sketches

Ezra Monroe (Ed) Allen

Ezra M. Allen, born August 13, 1895, married Dona Fisher who was born February 20, 1895. They were married December 2, 1918. They moved to Westfir June 1931 and worked for Westfir Lumber Company. They had six children, Naomi Allen Thurman, Ulas Allen, Robert Allen, Ann Allen Swaryck, Alta Allen Racy, Clarence Allen. Mr. Allen was Grand Marshal of the 1989 Tree Planting Festival parade.

Jeff Barbier

Jeff Barbier and Robin Kay McFarland were married July 9, 1988. Robin graduated Oakridge High School 1980. Robin was born April 27, 1962.

Marion Hugh Beard

Marion H. Beard married Patricia A. West in 1953. Their children are Marion Douglas Beard and Michael Edward Beard.

Richard Behr

Richard Behr, born September 15, 1919, and Helga Enkeboll, born February 14, 1915, married in 1943. They came to Oakridge in 1946 when Dick went to work as a forester for Pope & Talbot.

They had two children, Charles Alan and Diana Emilia Behr. Charles graduated O.S.U. in Meteorology in 1970 and married Cho Kyong Cha whom he met while in the army in Korea. They have two children, John Edward Behr and Julie Ann Behr. Diana graduated from Oregon College of Education at Monmouth.

While in Oakridge, Dick worked for Pope & Talbot as forester until 1953; and from 1953 to 1963, he owned and operated Gas Heat of Oakridge. He played in the very active softball league from 1948 to 1953, was a charter member of the Lions Club, serving as secretary and president. He was an active member of the Chamber of Commerce working many long, pleasant hours on the Tree Planting Festival. Dick spent four years on the City Council and enjoyed that, too. He helped build Circle Bar Golf Club and spent as many hours as possible playing there.

Helga and Dick both liked to ski and spent some time at Willamette Pass skiing with Don Temple and others.

Helga taught home economics during the 1946–47 school year in Oakridge. Another teacher who had been hired decided to leave and Helga soon learned why. In the classrooms there were two ranges — one was electric with a problem with oven temperature control and the other was a wood range (primitive for 1946).

There were two electric sewing machines and several treadle machines (also primitive). They were difficult to use because some of the treadles stuck and would jerk the fabric forward under the pressure foot. Since Helga knew how to handle the wood range and the treadle machines and the students cooperated, good results were had by all.

It should be remembered that new equipment was hard to come by so soon after World War Two.

Helga remembered that the only cement sidewalks in town were in front of the schools and that there were many eyesores of old wood sheds and outhouses near the main street in 1946. That, too, changed with the growth of the town in the late 1940's.

Victor Bjorling

Victor Bjorling, born 1907 in Sweden, his wife Ethel was born 1903. They lived in Westfir from 1944 to 1952 and their daughter Dorothy went to school there. Dorothy worked at Edward Hines Lumber Company in 1948.

Dorothy M. Bjorling married W.R. Knott and they had two daughters, Janet M. Knott (Jenkins) and Karen A. Knott (O'Hearn). Janet's children are Sandra Marie and Joby Ryan Jenkins. Karen's children are Russell and Samantha O'Hearn.

Dorothy Bjorling Knott lives in Monroe, Washington.

Steven T. Black

Steven T. Black married Emma Belle Pengra who was born in 1860, the daughter of Bynon J. Pengra. Steven and Emma were married in 1878. His home was Big Prairie. Emma was a sister of Mrs. James A. Walker and Mrs. George W. Larison who were residents of Big Prairie.

The Blakelys of Blakelyville

John Blakely, born in Dublin, Ireland, on June 20, 1829, stowed away on a boat when he was twelve years old and made his way to America. He brought his family to the Upper Willamette in about 1887.

They lived in a log cabin for about five years and then moved to the house that later became the Blakelyville Post Office.

John and his wife Isabelle had a large family. The children were William, Thomas, Joseph, Emmett, Frank, Stella, Ella, Jane, Flora and Elisabeth (Lizzie).

Postmasters at the Blakelyville Post Office were Martin Clark, Ella Michael, Joe Blakely and Mary Blakely. At the request of the railroad, the name of the Post Office was changed to Eula. Eula Post Office was named for Eula Blakely, the daughter of Joe Blakely. The railroad station at the same location was changed to Armet because of confusion with another Oregon place called Eola. The Post Office was discontinued in 1943.

John Blakely died in 1893. Before he died, he moved his family from the log cabin to a house and he had hop yards producing. Hop yards were a source of income for the owners and for the hop pickers who worked each fall to harvest the crop. Indians came from eastern Oregon to get work in the hop yards in the fall.

For forty years, John Blakely's descendants lived in the Blakelyville area. Then in the late 1940's, the Lookout Point Dam was built and the houses were torn down. Soon the land was covered with the water of the reservoir.

Walter Blakely

Walter Blakely worked on the old incline on the North Fork. Walter and Mattie Hebert were married June 21, 1918. Their children are Lawrence Blakely, Leona Blakely Wilcox and Bonnie Blakely Heimburger. Walter died in 1968 and Mattie died in 1984.

Georges F. Bouhey

Georges Bouhey, born October 5, 1911, at Pincher Creek, Alberta, Canada, and Artie Zoe McGill of Fall City, Washington, were married in 1932. Artie was born December 21, 1913.

Artie and Georges had two children, Joy D. (Lee) and Georges Maurice.

The family moved to Oakridge in 1946 and Georges built houses and the office building for Pope & Talbot. He was appointed Oakridge Justice of the Peace by Governor Robert Holmes. He served in that office from 1947 to 1953. He was also a city councilman for many years.

In 1953 he was hired by Ketchikan Pulp Company to design and build the logging community of Hollis, built on an island in southeast Alaska.

He returned to Oakridge in 1957 and bought Oakridge Builders Supply, which he owned and operated until he retired in 1974. In 1959, he supplied a number of prefabricated houses for Hollis, Alaska. He had an agreement with Howard Kissinger and Associates to construct and erect the homes. Bouhey supplied the lumber and Kissinger, Lloyd Howard and others built the sections in Oakridge, near the railroad. They went by rail to Tacoma, Washington, where the flatcars were loaded intact on barges and shipped to Alaska. At Ketchikan, they were loaded on another barge for Prince of Wales Island and hauled by truck to Hollis.

Georges went to Alaska to prepare the site and Kissinger and Howard went up to assemble the houses. They were complete in the spring of 1960.

After Georges retired, he grew and sold Christmas trees and was active in the Neighborhood Watch organization.

Artie has been active in Garden Club for many years and in 1979 she became a Master Judge of the Oregon Federation of Garden Clubs.

Georges died on December 30, 1988.

Joy D. Bouhey Lee and Ira Val Lee had two children — Martin Val Lee, born November 9, 1955, died in an auto accident July 25, 1976, and Brenda Joy Lee was born June 26, 1959, and married Scott Nelson August 27, 1988.

Georges M. Bouhey, a drummer with the Mason Williams band for a number of years, married Sharyle Anderson and has two children — Kristen, born in 1977, and Georges Joel, born in 1981.

Robert E. Brewer, Sr.

Robert Brewer, Sr., born December 9, 1919, in Rogers, Kentucky, moved to Oakridge in 1951. He married Genevieve Sims, born April 30, 1930, who moved to Oakridge in 1944. Bob was a sawyer at Pope & Talbot, then a sawmill superintendent until 1979. Genevieve and Bob have four children, Carolyn L., Karen Marie, Robert E., Jr., and Rodney A.

Robert E. Brewer, Jr., has two children, Cristopher and Shayla.

Waldo J. Campbell

Waldo Campbell, born June 10, 1915, and Irene Cooney, born April 10, 1916, were married on August 16, 1935. They moved to Oakridge in 1948 where Waldo and a partner built and operated the Oasis Tavern on First Street. Waldo was active in Lions Club, Oakridge Rod and Gun Club and served on the City Council.

Waldo sponsored a baseball team in the 1950's. The stands would be full of people. This was before television. Some of the ball players were: the Shorey brothers, Yeager, Kissinger, Simon, Fulton, Jenkins, Williams, LaBansky, Dutton, Reid, Bates and Priddy.

Irene was the daughter of Benjamin W. Cooney, an agronomist who was the first County Agent for Douglas County, Oregon. He was a graduate of the University of Nebraska.

Irene worked for a number of years in the Oakridge Insurance office of Ray Ramey. She was a member of the Oakridge Business and Professional Womens Club.

Irene and Waldo had two children, Sharon L. (Carlisle) and Joseph V. "Van." Sharon has three children, Gregory Filter, Kayla L. Filter and Amy E. Filter. Sharon is married to Robert L. Carlisle. Joseph Campbell is married to Leslie Perkins. They have a son Mark Thomas, and they live in Fairbanks, Alaska.

Gregory Filter and his wife Gina have two children, a daughter Lauren and a son Andrew. They are Irene's great grandchildren. Waldo Campbell died in 1972. Irene still lives in Oakridge.

Frank B. Chenoweth

Frank B. Chenoweth, born 1883 and died 1940, had a homestead on High Prairie and married Edith Holt November 22, 1904. They had one daughter Thelma Lucille, born 1908. Edith Chenoweth died in 1959.

James H. Chenoweth

James H. Chenoweth, born 1856 and died 1952, homesteaded on High Prairie and is the father of Frank Chenoweth.

Charles Edward Clark

Charles Edward (Ed) Clark was born in 1897 at Comstock Precinct in Douglas County, Oregon. He came to Oakridge with his family in 1910. Ed built the first garage in Oakridge which he operated for a couple of years before selling it to Larwence Hills. He then built another larger garage which he operated for thirteen years. Both of these garages were located on First Street in Oakridge. When the new highway was built in 1937, Ed built a new service station and garage on the highway.

In 1922 he married Louise Walker, daughter of a pioneer family. Louise was born in 1904 in Springfield, Oregon. Her parents were William and Olive Walker of Oakridge (Hazeldell at the time). Louise is the great granddaughter of Bynon J. Pengra, on her father's side of the family and the great granddaughter of Lucinda Sanford Orr on her mother's side of the family.

Louise Clark was chosen "Citizen of the Year" in 1953 for her outstanding work in heading a campaign that resulted in the establishment of the City Library. Governor Paul Patterson was on hand to make the presentation and speak of the work Louise had done for the library and the Garden Club.

Ed and Louise had one son, Dale Randal Clark, who was born in 1924.

Randal Clark owned Northwest Cable T.V. of Oakridge. Randal had three daughters, Dale, Cindy and Randie.

Charles E. Clark

Charles E. Clark, born in California in 1866, came to Oakridge in 1910. In 1895, he married Catherine D'Orsay who was born in 1875 in Providence, Rhode Island. Charles and Catherine came to Oakridge when construction of the railroad was in progress. They were the parents of eight children, Charles Edward (born 1897), William McKinley (born 1900), John Albert (born 1902, died 1956), Eula Mary (born 1905), Milton James (born 1907, died 1932), Maude Catherine (born 1909), Ellen Irene (born 1911) and their first child LeRoy (born 1896, died 1908). Charles died in Oakridge in 1939 and his wife Catherine died in 1944.

Earl H. Clark

Earl H. Clark, born 1919 in Curtin, Oregon, was a driver-mechanic for Oakridge Sand and Gravel. He married Ruth Hill in 1940. They have a daughter Judy Clark Page and a son Dennis Clark, a Vietnam veteran.

Harry Clark

Harry Clark, born June 9, 1921 in San Diego, California, and Barbara Tatro, born September 1, 1928, were married on June 23, 1948.

Harry and Barbara have two children, Stephen and Christine. Stephen married Sherryl Cornish and they have three children. Christine married Bobby Tillotson and they have four children.

Harry moved to Oakridge in September of 1946 after being hired by L.L. "Stub" Stewart three months after Pope & Talbot, Inc., purchased the Penn Tract of old growth Douglas fir timber and 32,234 acres of land. Harry was Timberlands and Logging Manager, Pope & Talbot, Inc., at Oakridge. Harry retired in 1986 after 40 years with the company.

Harry met his wife Barbara when he moved to Oakridge. Barbara died on July 17, 1986.

Hobart Aliska Clark

Hobart Aliska Clark, born August 17, 1910 in Eula, Oregon, was married in 1938 to Velma Luella Williams, born August 24, 1912, in Hopland, California.

Hobart grew up and received his education in Oakridge and served in the U.S. Army in World War Two. He owned and operated local business property. He was a partner with his brother Raymond Clark in the Oakridge Sand and Gravel Company.

Velma and Hobart had four children — Dwayne, Aulene, Mildred and Raymond M. Agee.

Irvin McClellan Clark

Irvin McClellan Clark, born 1904 in Curtin, Oregon, came to Oakridge in 1925. His wife was Olive Sutherlin, born 1905 at Mill City, Oregon. Their children included three sets of twins — Katherine (McClintock, born 1924), Irvin D. (born 1930), twins Flora M. (Pugh) and Donald R. (born 1932), twins Terry R. and Jerry R. (born 1936), Kenneth R. (born 1938), twins Larry G. and Gary D. (born 1940), Douglas M. (born 1945) and Gloria J. (born 1947). Mrs Clark died in 1955.

Martin Aliska Clark

Martin Aliska Clark, born February 14, 1880, was married in 1900 to Elvina Neyman, born February 24, 1884. Martin was a postmaster at Eula, Oregon. He died in 1931 in Eugene.

Martin and Elvina had eight children — Ethel Amelia, Irvin (Bud), Thomas Volney,

Bessie B., Hobart Aliska, Raymond C., Earl H. and Baby Clark.

Elvina married again after Martin died. She married Peter Pearson. Elvina died in 1943. Peter died in 1967.

Raymond C. Clark

Raymond C. Clark, born 1914 in Eula, Oregon, came to Oakridge in 1914. He married Dorothy Pearson in 1932. Raymond was co-owner of Oakridge Sand and Gravel. Their children are Allen R., Wayne E. and Dareld J. Clark.

Albert E. Clifford

Albert "Al" Clifford, born 1916, married Mary "Betty" Hugill. Betty was born in 1919 in Oregon. Al worked for 34 years for Southern Pacific Railroad as a traveling motor car repairman. He came to Oakridge in 1944 and the family followed in 1948. They lived in Woodburn, Oregon.

Al had a 1921 Model T sedan delivery that he drove in every tree planting parade until he died in the fall of 1984. He was Master of the High Prairie Grange for two years.

Betty worked as a cook for School District 76 for 12 years. She was Master, Secretary and H.E.C. Chairman for the Grange. She has been a valuable volunteer in many civic activities, receiving a Woman of the Year award from B.P.W.

Their children are John E. (born May 31, 1937), Patricia (Wells, born January 13, 1939), and Susan (Fields, born January 21, 1956).

John E. "Jack" Clifford

Jack Clifford, born 1937, married Tamaris Rogers, born 1939. Jack was a U.S. Forest Service construction engineer and then started his own company, Clifford Brushcutting. Tamaris is a realtor. They have three children — Sherene (Crager, born 1959), Brock (born 1961) and Gaye (Luna, born 1964). Brock Clifford works in Alaska for BLM.

Art Cooper

Art and Doris Cooper came to Oakridge in the 1940's to open a cabinet shop. Art had soon equipped many Upper Willamette kitchens with cabinets, and he made the charming rustic furniture for Kitson Springs. Made of peeled cedar and fir, this native furniture became a trademark of the resort.

While her husband was busy with building and cabinet making, Doris taught first grade at Oakridge School for six years. She then did substitute teaching for five more years.

They owned Coopers Craft Shop which was later known as The Trading Post.

Art served as a member of the Oakridge School Board, Oakridge Water Board, City Park Board, Lane County Park Board, Oakridge Chamber of Commerce and Lane County Chamber of Commerce. He received the Oakridge "Citizen of the Year" award in 1954. In presenting the award to Art, Dr. O. Meredith Wilson (then president of the University of Oregon) spoke of his unselfish donation of material and labor to build the park gates, his work on the Tree Planting Festival, Oakridge City Park program, Chamber of Commerce Information Center, and his many contributions to the work of civic betterment committees.

Doris, too, has been active in civic affairs and she served as president of the

Oakridge Parent Teacher Association and Upper Willamette Business and Professional Women's Club. She helped get the Tree Planting Festival off to a good start by serving as the first chairman for the 1953 festival.

Doris was born in 1908 in Grants Pass, Oregon. Her maiden name was Woolfolk. She is a graduate of Southern Oregon College and has attended summer sessions at the University of Oregon. She married Arthur E. Cooper on June 15, 1930. He was born in Ashland, Oregon, in 1907. He went to school in Ashland and worked as a cabinetmaker in Southern Oregon before coming to the Upper Willamette.

Al Crist

Al Crist, born September 21, 1919, in Milton, Washington, was married in 1938 to Katherine McKenzie, born October 14, 1919. They moved to Oakridge in 1952. Katherine and Al had three children — Donald J., Peggy and Dave.

Al worked for Hines Lumber Company for three years then started his own contract logging business. In 1975, Al and son Dave went to Alaska to help build the oil pipeline. They spent three years up there.

In 1989, Al and sons Don and Dave were back to contract logging around Oakridge. Al says, "I love it here and wouldn't want to live anywhere else."

Donald married Donna Baird and they had two sons, John and James. Donna works in the Oakridge School District office.

Peggy married Howard Phearson. Her children are Vonnie and Howard.

Dave married Nancy Stears and has two children, Katheryn and Tony.

George C. Crook

George Crook, born July 31, 1906, in Lumberton, Mississippi, and Claire Thomen, born September 26, 1910, were married August 8, 1942.

Claire taught first grade in Oakridge for 28 years and taught in Columbia County for 15 years before moving to Oakridge. Claire graduated from the University of Oregon. She and George moved to Oakridge in 1948. George was head saw filer for Pope & Talbot for 35 years. He set up the saw filing room when Pope & Talbot first came to Oakridge.

Dick Culbertson

Dick Culbertson, born August 13, 1935, in Seattle, Washington, married Mae Bowerman, born May 7, 1936, in Eugene, Oregon. They were married in 1957, lived in Oakridge from 1960 to 1963 and from 1980 to present. Dick was a silviculturist for the U.S. Forest Service until he retired in 1985. He then started an appliance repair business. Dick was elected to be mayor of Oakridge in 1986 and was sworn in January of 1987.

Mae's father worked seasonally for the U.S.F.S. in the early 1920's. He worked under the direction of "Mac" McFarland. He was a lookout on Saddle Blanket Mountain. He said that when a mule wouldn't get in the truck, "Mac" just picked him up and put him in!

Dick and Mae have four children, Diane E., Joanne L., Alice E. and Mark R. Diane married Alan Peterson and they have two children, Emily J. and James A. Peterson.

Dick and Mae are both involved in community affairs, Chamber of Commerce, Tree Planting Festival, Waldo Days, as well as work with the Church of the Nazarene.

Lyle Porter Cunningham

Lyle Cunningham, born February 16, 1939, in Olympia, Washington, moved to Oakridge in 1948. Lyle married Mildred L. Clark, born July 23, 1945, in Westfir, Oregon. They were married on May 10, 1969.

Lyle worked for Pope & Talbot and Mildred works for Image Business Forms, Inc.

They have two children, Lisa Pauleen and Lyle Phillip. Lisa went to school in Oakridge and to college in Eugene. She married Michael J. Evans and has one child Nikki Luella. Lyle Phillip went to school in Oakridge and to college in Idaho.

John Davidson

John Davidson, born November 12, 1918, in Doyan, North Dakota, married Myrtle Price in 1942. They lived in the Oakridge area for over 40 years. John and his sons have been in the road construction business.

They have three sons. Jerald Davidson married Shirley Bottoms, Roy Davidson married Diane Dalton and David Davidson married Leslie LaDuke.

Bert E. Davis

Bert E. Davis was born in 1914. He was a U.S. Forest Service employee, a rancher and a logger. He married Iola Dunning in 1940 in Eugene, Oregon. Bert served on the Oakridge School Board and has been active in other civic affairs. Bert and Iola are the parents of Ann Jeanette and Roberta. Ann Jeanette Davis, M.D., married Richard Reindollar, M.D. Roberta (Robin) Davis has a B.S. degree with R.N.

Alvin P. Dean

Alvin Dean, born January 11, 1925, in Goshen, Oregon, and Viola "Vickie" Horner, born October 3, 1925, in Corvallis, Oregon, were married on March 23, 1947. They lived in Oakridge from 1947 to 1985.

Alvin and Vickie had four children, Loretta Rae, Gary R., Mary C. and Robert A.

Alvin served in the Air Force during World War Two. After he got home, he attended the University of Oregon where he met Vickie. In 1950, he was recalled to serve in the Air Force during the Korean War. He came home again in 1951 and went to work for Pope & Talbot as a millwright. He was medically retired in 1984. He died in Bend in 1985.

Alvin and Vickie were very active in the community. They were members of V.F.W., American Legion, P.T.A., Moose Lodge and other organizations.

They were both active in Boy Scouts of America serving in many capacities. Alvin received the Silver Beaver Award in 1969 for his outstanding service, and Vickie received the Silver Fawn Award in 1974.

Howard R. Dean

Howard R. Dean, born September 7, 1920, married Elizabeth Wert in 1940. They had two children, Penny Lou and Terry R. Dean. Howard served in the Marine Corps during World War Two. While he lived in Oakridge, he was a student, worked for the Forest Service and worked in logging and construction. His parents were Orville and Freda Dean.

Orville B. Dean

Orville Dean, born October 9, 1894, married Freda Dillard in 1919. Their children are Howard, Flora and Alvin.

Robert Allen Dean

Robert Dean, born September 12, 1955, and Momikai E. Mount, born September 19, 1955, in Yokohama, Japan, were married in 1975. They had both lived in Oakridge while they grew up. Robert is the son of Alvin and Vicki Dean and Momikai is the daughter of Clyde and Fumiko Mount.

William C. Dentel

William Dentel, born September 15, 1929, in Echo, Oregon, and Phyllis Fleischman, born May 18, 1928, were married August 23, 1952, in Corvallis, Oregon. They moved to Oakridge in 1963. Bill was teaching until 1976. He then started a construction business. Phyllis is a teacher-librarian at Oakridge High School.

Their children are Thomas William, born in 1953, and Stephen Dale, born in 1955. Thomas graduated from Oakridge High School, attended LCC and OSU, married Karen Woolery and they have two children, Michelle and Niki. Thomas is Head of Maintenance for Harrisburg Elementary and Junior High Schools in Harrisburg, Oregon.

Stephen graduated from Oakridge High School, attended the Air Force Academy and OSU, graduated in business and computer science. He has been with Hewlett-Packard since graduation. He married Vicki Z'berg and they live in Vancouver, Washington.

Valere Marcel DeVogele, R.P.

Valere M. DeVogele, born 1953, married Beth McFarland in August of 1977. They have two children, Alisha R. and Valere M. (Marc).

Neil E. Diess, M.D.

Neil Diess was born September 8, 1927, to Ivan and Iris Diess of Kansas City, Missouri. Ivan and Iris lived in Oakridge and he worked at the mill in Westfir until 1958.

Neil married Lois Mae Croner in 1946. She was the daughter of Charles and Mildred Croner who moved to Oakridge in 1923 and had a drugstore until 1952. Mildred Croner Blair was the Oakridge Postmaster for 27 years. She and Charles were active in community affairs, serving on the school board, and Charles was mayor of Oakridge in the mid 1940's. They were in the Masonic Lodge and Eastern Star and American Legion and its auxiliary.

Neil was a physician in Oakridge from 1955 to 1958.

Neil and Lois have three children, Richard C., Karen L. and Susan C.

Karen Diess Tilley has two children, Alyson Blair Tilley and Kirk John Tilley.

Andy J. Draper

Andy Draper was born February 8, 1907, in Mt. Pleasant, Utah. Margaret Bunnell, born February 20, 1913, and Andy were married on August 6, 1936. They came to Oakridge in 1947. They had four children, Jerald, Susan (Rasmussan), Phillip and Melvin.

Andy was the station agent for Southern Pacific at Oakridge. Margaret died in 1962 and Andy in 1977. Their son Phillip died in 1963.

Jerald has three children and lives in Hood River. Susan has four boys and lives in Eugene. Melvin and his wife Sharon Kenyon Draper have two boys, Erik and

Brian. They live in Oakridge. Melvin likes to hunt and fish. He sets traplines in the winter in the Oakridge area. He has lived here all his life and has worked for Pope & Talbot.

Charles Marion Dunning

Charles Marion Dunning, born in 1870 in Iowa, came to the Oakridge area in 1908. He married Mercy Holt in 1895. He farmed and worked for the U.S. Forest Service. The children of Charles and Mercy Dunning are: Harold Holt Dunning (born 1897, died 1898), Ralph M. (born 1898, died 1898) and twin Raymond L. (born 1898) and Robert R. (born 1905).

Raymond L. Dunning

Raymond L. Dunning, born in 1898 in Iowa, came to the Oakridge area in 1908 and married Clara Prokop on May 18,1919, in Eugene, Oregon. They were the parents of Iola M. and Joanna.

Robert R. Dunning

Robert R. Dunning, born in 1905 in Iowa, came to the Oakridge area in 1908. He married Anna Jeske in 1933 in Oakridge, Oregon. They are the parents of Robert Charles Dunning.

Edward L. Eaton

Edward L. Eaton, born in 1892 in Jasper, Oregon, is the son of Edward Warren Eaton and Dora Glaspey Eaton. Grandfather Will Eaton ran the ferry at Jasper. Ed worked for the old Hyland Logging Company in the Fall Creek area, then farmed at Landax and moved to Oakridge when the Landax area was taken for the site of Lookout Point Reservoir.

Edward married Edith Cain in 1918. She was born at Landax in 1901 and is the daughter of Methias Cain and Margaret Lewis Cain. Edith's mother's family, the Lewis family, came to the Willamette Valley in 1853 by wagon train.

Edward and Edith Eaton have two daughters, Thelma Eaton Hamilton and Genevieve Eaton Rutherford.

James Louis Flock

James Louis Flock was born in 1882 in Cow Creek, Oregon. He married Lina A. Warner in 1906 in Eugene, Oregon. Lina was born in 1886 in Big Prairie (Oakridge). Her parents were Frank and Susan Warner, pioneers of the Upper Willamette area. James and Lina spent a year in southeastern Washington and then returned to Oakridge where they lived until 1935. Then they moved to Fall Creek and after that to Powell Butte in 1942. They both died at Powell Butte — Lina in 1956 and Louis in 1964.

James and Lina were the parents of two children — Mildred, born in 1910, and Orlo Alva, born in 1913.

In 1927 when Lewis A. McArthur was writing *Oregon Geographic Names,* he corresponded with Mrs. Lina A. Flock of Oakridge and she supplied him with information on the origin of some of the local geographic names. Lina's father Frank Warner with his Indian friend Charlie Tufti explored much of the high country around Oakridge.

William Flock

William Flock came to Oakridge in 1910. His wife was Margaret Craydon Flock. William died in Oakridge in 1920 and Margaret died in 1924. They were the parents of James Louis (born 1882), Mary Ellen (Tiller, born 1867), Alva Willard (born 1869), Sara Edna (Raymond, born 1871), Samuel L. (born 1874, married Ida Chaney), Clara M. (born 1876, married Henry Horton), Emma N. (born 1879, married Dr. Herbert Higgins), William P. (born 1885, married Lora Sharp), Ada M. (born 1888, married Marion Lewis) and Jesse E. (born 1891, married Viola Osborn).

Lauren A. Gale

Lauren A. Gale was born in New York in 1895. He came to Oakridge in 1926. He was an engineer for Southern Pacific Railroad. He owned and operated Gales Trailer Court, later known as Salmon Creek Trailer Court. Gale Street was named for him. He had one son, Lauren H. Gale.

A.E. Gerimonte

The name Gerimonte was well known around Westfir and Oakridge for many years. Gerry was a long-time employee of the Edward Hines Lumber Company. In Westfir, he was a purchasing agent and personnel manager. When he became public relations manager, he and his wife Esther moved to Eugene.

He was active in many civic affairs, including Lane County Chamber of Commerce, Oakridge-Westfir Chamber of Commerce, Lions Club and the Oakridge Catholic Church. He was famous for his spaghetti feeds for fund raising for his church.

Israel J. Gray

Israel J. Gray, born in 1840 in Armstrong County, Pennsylvania, came to the Upper Willamette in 1882 when Oakridge was called Big Prairie. His wife was the former Theresa Orr who was born in 1856 at Waltham, Illinois. Israel and Theresa were the parents of two girls, Daisy Lee who married George Hebert and Olive May who married William S. Walker in 1903.

Israel was a Sergeant-Major with the 61st Regiment of the Pennsylvania Volunteers in the Civil War. After the war, he came west to Illinois where he met his wife. When their youngest child was five months old, they started for Oregon. They came by rail to San Francisco and by boat from there to Portland. When they finally reached Big Prairie, they took a preemption land claim on High Prairie; then in 1890, they homesteaded on Gray's Creek south of the river. Later they bought the old Ashley homestead and lived there for many years. The house they lived in on the Ashley place was located where the new M.R. Holst house has been built. (See *Biographical Sketches, Thomas Orr*)

Stanley Ira Gray

Stanley Ira Gray was born in Thurston, Oregon, in 1895. He married Margaret Farrell in 1915. They moved to a farm in Landax in 1921 where they kept a dairy and raised alfalfa, corn and beef cattle until 1944 when their farm was taken as the site of Lookout Point Reservoir. Then they moved to Oakridge and Stanley worked as a millwright at Westfir Mill from 1944 to 1954. Stanley was a member of the Lowell School Board for 15 years. He and Margaret were members of Lowell Grange for many years, and they made the Grange exhibits for the Lane County Fair many times.

Margaret Farrell Gray was born in Wyoming in 1889. She taught school in Oregon for 41 years at Thurston, Landax, Unity, Dexter and Westfir. She also taught 4-H Club groups for over 20 years.

The Grays are the parents of a son and daughter, Francis Gray of Silver Springs, Maryland, and Elizabeth Gray Haralson of Eugene. They also have five grandchildren.

Max Gosnell

Max Gosnell, born 1909 in Canada, and Florence Henry, born 1906, were married in 1944. They had three children, Norman Jerginson, Sandra (Pyles) and Florence Gosnell.

Max and Florence moved here from Clatskanine, Oregon, in 1964. Max worked for Pope & Talbot for ten years before he retired. He has been curator for the Oakridge Museum for 10 years. He says that being curator is very rewarding. Florence has been active in museum work in many capacities.

Max A. Greer *(written by Max Greer, August 1989)*

My mother Georgia Greer, my sister Onata and I came to Oakridge from New Mexico in 1928 after my father died. We arrived on the train and came into the town after it had been raining. The streets were very muddy and deeply rutted. My uncle Dan Brown who had lived here for a couple of years met us and took us to his little house on East First Street. My mother, sister and I soon moved to the McAtee Hotel on First Street because the house was so small. Mother worked in Mrs. Neal's restaurant which was located on First Street near the present law office. During the war she worked for the railroad in the roundhouse as an oiler.

About 1931, Uncle Dan leased the McFarland Ranch and we all moved out there to the old Orr house which was situated about where the present Harvey McFarland house stands.

Onata and I had to walk to school, of course, and we always cut across what is now the golf course. It was then the Ash Ranch and a cow pasture which we had to cross. They were very curious cows and they often chased us as we ran as hard as we could for the fence. I carried a pocket full of rocks to fend off the old bull and managed to discourage him quite a few times.

After a couple of years, we moved to a ranch on High Prairie and lived in a house just south of the Crispin house. A school bus took us to school and back, but if we wanted to take part in any extracurricular activities we had to walk home at night. I remember that the only way I could find my way was to stay on the road, which I did in the dark by looking up to see the openings in the trees. If I got off the road, I'd be lost. I would run and walk and make it home in about an hour. Lots of times I thought a cougar or some animal was following me, but I never had one attack me.

I graduated from Oakridge High School in 1935. On graduation day, two cousins and I caught a freight train to Eugene just for a lark intending to be back by late afternoon. We caught the wrong one coming back and when it started down toward Roseburg we had to jump off and wait for another. By the time we got back to Oakridge, it was almost time for graduation exercises so there was no time to go home. Fortunately, the high school principal, Gilbert Sprague, was about my size and he loaned me a suit to wear to graduation.

After graduation, I drove a school bus, worked as librarian at the high school and then got a job at Richter's dairy. After that, I clerked in a grocery store on the corner of First Street across from the present Uptown Market. When the tunnel was being built on Highway 58, I worked as a carpenter's helper in the tunnel. Later I was a whistle punk for the Westfir Lumber Company under Scott Butler.

In 1939, I married Velma Weaver of Myrtle Creek. In 1940, we moved to San Francisco where I went to business college at night while working days in a knitting company. During the war, I worked as a welder in the shipyards. Our daughter Linda was born in 1942. We came back to Oakridge in 1946 and I worked with my brother-in-law, Fred Baxter, building houses. Later, we had a portable sawmill with Bruce Haralson for about three years. Then I worked for Pope & Talbot on housing construction, bridge building, etc. In 1955, I began as a mechanic and welder in the logging operation for Pope & Talbot and worked there for 24 years.

In 1961, I lost my wife and daughter Sandra in an automobile accident. She was then fourteen years old.

In 1962, I married June Denison, a school teacher in Eugene.

In 1964, we adopted our son Randy at age 7, and three years later we adopted our daughter Joyce, also at age 7. In another three years we adopted Sheila at age 8 and three years later adopted Tammy who was also 8.

Linda married Murray Johnson in 1964. They have two daughters — Laura and Dinah who are in college. The Johnsons live in Milwaukee, Wisconsin, where he works for the regional office of the Forest Service.

Randy married Mary Heywood. They have two daughters Sunny and Kristen and a son Aaron. They live in Dublin, California, where Randy is employed by a dry cleaning firm.

Joyce married Mark Lundbom in 1981. They have two daughters Melissa and Amanda and two sons Jonathan and Devin. Their home is in Springfield, Oregon.

Sheila married Tony Hammock in 1983. They have one daughter Jessica. They were divorced in 1985. Sheila married Brian Keller in 1989 and they live in Oakridge.

Tammy married Mike Tabor in 1989. They have a son Bryan and a daughter Heather. They live in Oakridge.

Isaac Hamner

Isaac Hamner was Postmaster of the Tiptop Post Office near Hill's Creek in 1895. His wife's name was Angelina.

Walter G. Hamner

Walter G. Hamner was born in 1869 and died in 1949. His wife Daisy Bell Hebert was born in 1882 and died in 1965. They were the parents of Carl (born 1901, died 1931), Ruby (born 1904, married Roy Bolton), Amy (born 1906, married David Biles), Dale (born 1908, married Lucille Praces), Clare (Dude, born 1910, died 1948), Kenneth (born 1914, wife Joyce), and Evelyn (born 1917, married Asel Walker). Walter Hamner homesteaded on High Prairie and served on the school board. Daisy was a school clerk.

Paul Hankins

Paul Hankins and his wife Irene have lived in Oakridge for 35 years where he was employed at Pope & Talbot for 17 years and she was employed at First National Bank for 15 years. They celebrated their 50th wedding anniversary on August 12, 1984. They have two children, Richard Hankins and Paula Hankins Bergeson.

Orvel Hansen, Sr.

Orvel Hansen, born November 16, 1918, at Hebo, Oregon, and Evelyn Walters, born September 20, 1921, were married and moved to Westfir when housing was built at Camp 6. Orvel stayed at the Westfir bunkhouse until a house at the camp was available for the family. They were the third family to move to the Camp 6 housing. Tweedys and Hookers were first. Orvel was a log truck driver, cat operator and shovel operator for Hines Lumber Company.

They had three sons, Orvel, Jr., Fredrick and Burt.

Orvel, Jr., married Pamela Henderson. Their children are Wendy Ann and Ryan Joel. Orvel, Jr., worked at Pope & Talbot until they sold in 1989.

Fredrick married Linda Ottinger and they have two children, Heidi Sue and Zachary. Fredrick teaches at Sabin High School and lives in Portland, Oregon.

Burt Hansen lives in Oakridge and works for TR&M Logging. He has a daughter Amy.

All three Hansen boys attended Oakridge schools.

Evelyn worked at the Oakridge Post Office for many years. She started there when Mildred Croner Blair was postmaster.

Charles E. Hebert

Charles E. Hebert was born in 1876 in Wisconsin. He moved to the Oakridge area in 1889. He was a carpenter and farmer, played "fiddle" for dances, cut hair and served on the High Prairie School Board. He married Jennie M. Holt in 1910. Jennie was born in 1885 in Iowa and came to the Oakridge area in 1909. She served as clerk on the High Prairie School Board.

Their children were Gladys (born 1911, married Gene J. Lavoy), Myrle (born 1913, married Maurice [Mike] Lee), Elsie (born 1914, married Jesse Davies), Charles (born 1916, died 1918), Frieda (born 1918, married Herbert [Bud] Lee), Ruth (born 1919, married Ben J. Bensen), Glenn E. (born 1921, married LaVelle Henderson), Hazel (born 1923, married M.C. [Bud] Vearrier) and Cleo (born 1925, married Willard Williams).

Clarence Hebert

Clarence Hebert, born 1902 on High Prairie, and Rigmore Johnson, born 1908, were married in 1932.

Clarence was one of George Hebert's sons. Clarence farmed and did sawmill work for 35 years. In the late 1920's, he bucked wood for steam logging donkeys.

Rigmore taught school in Westfir and Oakridge for 33 years.

Rigmore and Clarence had two children, Joanne (Garcia) and Edward Hebert. Joanne and Tom Garcia have one son, Troy. Edward and his wife have three children, Curtis, Leanne and Stacy. Clarence had a brother Ernest who died in 1971 and a sister Ethel (Singletary) who died in 1936.

George E. Hebert

George E. Hebert, born in 1869 in Wisconsin, came to Hazeldell in 1889 and married Daisy Lee Gray in January of 1899. She was born in 1876 in Illinois and came to the Upper Willamette area in 1882. The couple took a homestead on High Prairie. He farmed and served on the school board. They were the parents of Ethel, born November of 1899 and married John Singletary; Clarence R., born 1902 and married Rigmore Johnson; and Ernest, born 1903 and did not marry.

Harry Hebert

Harry Hebert, born July 2, 1873, came to the Oakridge area with his family in 1889. He never married and he died in 1949.

James Clark Hebert

James Clark Hebert, born January 17, 1871, married Alberta Patrick. He died in 1955.

Lewis Hebert

Lewis Hebert, born October 28, 1866, came to the Oakridge area in 1889. He died in 1943.

Peter Hebert

Peter Hebert, born May 29, 1839, in Quebec, Canada, married Martha Clark who was born in 1841. They came to the Oakridge area in 1889. Peter and Martha were the parents of Vertie (Bert), Lewis, George, Harry, James, Charles, William and Daisy.

Vertie (Bert) Hebert

Vertie (Bert) Hebert, born March 12, 1863, married Della Holesclaw. He owned a ranch where Pope & Talbot is now. Hazeldell post office was in the Bert Hebert home for many years. Bert died in 1928. Bert and Della had ten children — LeRoy (born 1893), Virgil (born 1896), Harry (born 1900), Claude (born 1902), Darrell (born 1905), Boyd (born 1907), Faye (born 1910), Margery (born 1912), Clifford (born 1914) and Delbert (born 1916).

William Hebert

William Hebert, born November 17, 1879, in Kansas, came to Oakridge in 1889. He worked for the Forest Service and was a logger. He married Nellie R. Holt in 1910. Nellie was born in 1890 in Mt. Pleasant, Iowa, and came to Oakridge in 1908. She finished high school and business college and was the first teacher hired after High Prairie School District was organized. She was owner and operator of the first cleaning and pressing shop in Oakridge. The couple had two daughters, Dorothy June and Vera Margaret.

Stanley Edward Heinz

Stanley E. Heinz, born 1953, married Jean McFarland, R.D., June 1977. They have three children — Stephanie A., Courtney J. and Erin Murphy.

Dale E. Helikson, J.D.

Dale E. Helikson, born August 12, 1920, in Eugene, Oregon, and Mary Kathryn Taylor, born August 25, 1920, in Junction City, Oregon, were married in 1943 and moved to Oakridge in 1948.

Dale was the first attorney-at-law with a private practice in the Upper Willamette area. He was Oakridge city attorney for 30 years, Oakridge School Board attorney for 25 years and Lowell city attorney for 15 years.

Dale was Medical Administrative Officer in World War Two and Korean War, member Oregon and Lane County Bar Associations, Oakridge City Beautification chairman (winning Small Cities Award twice). He was a board member and active volunteer for United Methodist Church, officer in many capacities for Oakridge Chamber of Commerce, member Audubon Society, Oakridge Museum President, 1969 Citizen of the Year, Lay Speaker of United Methodist Church and Laubach Tutor.

Mary K. has a BS 1942 University of Oregon with RN and PHN certificate. She has been United Methodist Women conference officer seven years, a board member and active volunteer for United Methodist Church, church school teacher, Methodist choir member, health clinic volunteer, Oakridge museum member and volunteer, 1977 Citizen of the Year, Girl Scout leader and organizer, cultural arts chairman of Home Extension (bringing four historical documentary plays to Oakridge), co-producer of *Oakridge Yesterday*, lay speaker of United Methodist Church and Laubach Tutor.

Dale and Mary K. had five children — Mary Alice, Susan Kay, Hubert Taylor, Beth Ann and Helen Jean.

Mary Alice Helikson, born July 9, 1945, is a pediatric surgeon and professor at the University of Missouri Health Science Center. Her husband is Brian Thomas. They have two children, Jocelyn and Lincoln.

Susan Kay, born April 4, 1948, is a teacher and children's librarian. Her husband is Rod Swanson and they have two children, Jeffrey and Joshua.

Hubert T. Helikson, born August 1, 1950, married Martha Pauly. He graduated from the University of Oregon with a Masters from Marylhurst in 1987. He is a distributor of Professional Pharmaceuticals.

Beth Ann, born September 18, 1956, is a teacher, legal secretary and office manager. Her husband is Norman Ritz. They have two boys, Reece and Neil.

Helen Jean, born February 7, 1962, is an agricultural engineer and a master's student at the University of Florida. She spent 27 months as a member of the Peace Corps in Haiti. She was chosen Future Citizen of the Year in 1979.

John Hill

John Hill was born in 1833 in Clark County, Kentucky. In 1856, he married Phoebe Warfield who was born in 1839 in Missouri. They had one son William James (Billy) born at Bunker Hill near Albany, Oregon, in 1857.

The Hill family came to Big Prairie (Oakridge) in 1866 and John went to work for Jim Sanford. He was a blacksmith. On Christmas Day, 1867, neighbors helped "raise" the house on the homestead, which was later the site of Hills Creek Dam.

John carried mail on horseback and his home was a post office from 1882 to 1885. They also "kept travel" as their home was on the Old Military Road. On an early map in *Walling's History of Lane County*, published in 1884, the Hill house is the only one shown east of Lowell although there were other houses in Big Prairie at that time which were older than the Hill home.

In 1906, John Hill died and was buried on the homestead. The place where he was buried is now the John Hill Memorial Cemetery.

In 1917, the Hill house burned and "Aunt Phoebe" and her son Billy moved to Alsea, Oregon. Phoebe died at Alsea in 1927 and Billy, who never married, died there in 1929.

Cornelius J. Hills

Cornelius Hills, born 1818 in New York, came to Oregon in 1847. He married Sophronia Briggs of Missouri in 1850. He brought his bride and relatives to Oregon in 1851. Their children were Jessie (Humphrey), Henrietta (Jacoby), Mary (Smith), Elijah, Joel, Sheridan, John and Jasper. The town of Jasper was named for Jasper Hills.

Jasper Hills

Jasper Hills, born 1859 in Oregon, married Flora Neet who was born in 1859 and whose family lived in Fall Creek, Oregon. They married about 1878 and moved to the Oakridge area at the turn of the century. They built a home and hunting lodge on Hill's Creek called the Bear's Den. Jasper was a hunter, trapper and logger.

Jasper and Flora had seven children — Fred, Roy, Charlie, Jessie (Stewart), Grace (Walker), Hallie (Huntington) and Lawrence (born April 27, 1902).

Lawrence Dan Hills

Lawrence Hills lived most of his life in the Upper Willamette country. He loved the area and contributed much to the community.

Lawrence worked for the U.S. Forest Service starting in 1917 and as a timber-faller in the woods in the early 20's. He enlisted in the U.S. Army in 1942 and after his service with the 14th Armored Division, he was married to Wilma Hamilton at Portland in 1945.

Until his retirement, Lawrence owned the Chevrolet dealership which he started on a shoestring during the depression years. Always active in community affairs, Lawrence worked on many committees, including the ambulance board (he owned the first ambulance in Oakridge, a 1929 Pierce Arrow), the park board and the foreign student committee. He served as Mayor of Oakridge from 1959 to 1967, was named Citizen of the Year in 1956 and received an award as one of the outstanding civic leaders of America in 1968.

In 1970, he constructed a reproduction of the original cabin of Eugene Skinner, the founder of Eugene, which stands in Skinner's Butte Park in Eugene. He built a second cabin in Greenwaters Park in Oakridge. His third was built for his two granddaughters and was trucked to their home on Bainbridge Island, Washington.

A lover of the outdoors and conservation, a lasting monument to his tireless energy is Greenwaters Park, near Oakridge, where he spent hundreds of volunteer hours.

Lawrence has left a fine legacy to the community of Oakridge. Each year he took the fourth grade classes on a field trip, explaining points of historic interest and bringing the past to life for the youngsters. He wrote a book about the Upper Willamette, *Tales from the Hills*.

Wilma and Lawrence had one son, Larry. He and his wife Carol have two daughters, Heide and Molly. They live in Washington.

Lawrence died February 9, 1989, at the age of 86.

Earl D. Holeman

Earl Holeman, born August 28, 1912, at Tacoma, Washington, married Dorothy Johnson, born January 30, 1920. They married in 1939 and moved to Oakridge the same year.

Earl was a section foreman for Southern Pacific Railroad. They called Oakridge home but spent from 1942 to 1952 moving from job to job in the railroad outfit cars. During that time, Earl spent 2½ years in service during World War Two. Earl worked for the railroad for 45 years on several different jobs. Earl and Dorothy built a house in Oakridge and lived in the same house for 37 years. Earl died in 1983.

Earl's stepfather was the first section foreman at Wicopee in 1927. His name was J.W. Jones. Years later, from 1952 to 1958, Earl was section foreman at Wicopee.

Dorothy and Earl had one daughter, Pamela Sue (Hensley) born in 1942. They had one granddaughter, Ramona Reed Schafer and two great granddaughters, Marissa Renee and Mikaela Kristine. Pamela went to school in Oakridge, graduating in 1960. Ramona went to grade school in Oakridge for a few years.

Dorothy worked for Hines Lumber Company and other businesses in the Oakridge area. She started the Nutrition Program for seniors in Oakridge and has been a volunteer worker for that program and for the Oakridge Museum as well as other things that benefit the people of the Upper Willamette. She is a member of the Oakridge Christian Church.

Maurice R. Holst

Maurice (Maurie) R. Holst and Anna (Effie) Holst moved to Oakridge in 1948. Here they started Holst Construction.

Maurie got his start by building block buildings in the Oakridge area, then service stations throughout Western Oregon. He built his first bridge over Salt Creek just east of Oakridge in the late 1950's.

From 1960 until 1985, Holst Construction built over one hundred bridges throughout the state of Oregon. In the Upper Willamette area, these would include: two bridges on the Dexter Lake Causeway, three bridges in the North Fork watershed including the access bridge to Hemlock, three bridges in the Salmon Creek watershed and three in the Hills Creek watershed.

Maurie did not confine himself solely to bridges. In 1959, he worked on the pressure tunnel on the lower east side of Hills Creek Dam. In 1965, he rebuilt the Hines Lumber Company log dam which was washed out by the 1964 flood. In 1968, he built the Oakridge sewage treatment plant. In 1969, he refurbished the covered bridge for Hines in Westfir. In 1972, he developed a system for lifting bridges to meet new specifications in highway construction. He raised 22 bridges on the I-5 corridor from 1972 to 1985.

Maurie was also active in community affairs. He served numerous terms on the Oakridge City Council and many other committees.

Maurie was injured on the job site in the North Santa Clara area when a crane came in contact with a power line. He died five weeks later on September 14, 1985, having never revived from a coma. He was survived by his wife Effie, sons Carson and Leland, and daughter Judy Wegge.

On October 21, 1987, on a flight from Oakridge to Florence, Oregon, Carson

Holst's plane crashed killing Carson, his mother Effie and Darlinda (Suzie) Taylor. The only survivor was Carson's small daughter Aubrey.

Leland Holst and Amy Bolin were married on December 20, 1986. Leland has dissolved the family business. The completed projects are a memorial to the builder.

Maurie Holst, Holst Construction, 1985.

Henry Holt

Henry Holt, born 1904, and Florence Miller, born 1915, were married in 1944. They have two daughters, Barbara (Schmidt) and Sharon (Kutch), City Recorder for Oakridge.

Henry came to Oakridge in 1923 and worked for the U.S. Department of Agriculture until retirement. He was President of the Upper Willamette Pioneer Association from 1960 to 1976. Florence was the Oakridge Museum curator from 1961 to 1976. Henry was President of the Forestvale Cemetery for many years. They worked with the Oakridge Museum in the early years of growth.

John C. Holt

John C. Holt, born October 8, 1880, in Iowa, came to the Upper Willamette in 1909 and married Emilie Hein. Their children are Helen (born 1912), Harold (born 1913) and Lucille (born 1922).

Randolph Holt

Randolph Holt, born March 12, 1847, in Quebec, Canada, married Mary Vincent who was born in Iowa on September 23, 1854. They were the parents of William, Bertha, Mercy (Mertie), Gertrude, John, Jennie, Edith, Nellie, Alice and Florence. The family came to the Oakridge area in 1908.

Donald Spencer Hughey

Donald Hughey, born February 22, 1919, at Lewistown, Montana, and Marjorie Chaplin, born April 22, 1923, were married in 1942. They had two daughters, Sandra Louise (Hise) and Marsha Anne. They have three grandchildren, Donald Spencer Hughey Parks, Kerry Anne Hughey Parks and Kyle Lane Rettinger.

Donald and Marjorie were the original owners and operators of the Sportsman Cafe in Oakridge. They operated it from 1947 to 1955. While they were in Oakridge, Don was President of the Chamber of Commerce when the first Tree Planting Festival was held. He also served as Lions Club President.

They served coffee and donuts for the April 1948 grand opening of Pope & Talbot and again when the First National Bank opened in Oakridge with Cap Ricks the manager.

Judson E. Hughey and his wife Anna Marie Spencer Hughey were co-owners of the Sportsman Cafe with Don and Marjorie. Judson and Anna were both born in 1886.

Donald is deceased. Marjorie married Roy L. Bradley in December 1975 and he died in June 1976. She lives in Winchester Bay, Oregon.

Essie Parker Hugill

Essie Parker Hugill was born in 1890. She moved to Oakridge in the early 1950's and operated a stationery and office supply store and dispatched cab for Vern Williams. She was the granddaughter of Oregon pioneer Samuel Franklin Parker who was active in the formation of the Territorial and State Governments. He also led several wagon trains from Missouri to Oregon.

Her daughters Betty Clifford and Dorothy Bacon have lived in Oakridge. Her sons James and Al lived in the area and son John lived in Seattle.

Percy Humphrey

Percy Nobel Humphrey was born in 1913 at Fall Creek and came to the Oakridge area in 1926. He married Thelma Davis in 1934. She was born at Deer Park, Washington, in 1917 and came to Oakridge in 1933.

Thelma, a nurse, worked at the Oakridge Clinic and at the doctor's office in Westfir. She worked with doctors Varney, Harris, Poole and Hunsaker.

Percy was a steam fitter and power house operator at Edward Hines Lumber Company at Westfir.

He is a direct descendant of Agnes Stewart Warner who kept a diary as she came to Oregon with the "Lost Wagon Train" of 1853. Agnes and her husband Tom

Warner had a son George Warner who had a daughter Tracy. Tracy Warner married Stanley Humphrey and they were the parents of Percy Humphrey. Percy is a fourth generation Oregonian.

Percy and Thelma were parents of three children, Jeanette (Mrs. Paul) Hodgdon of Hillsboro, Oregon, Judith (Mrs. Kenneth) Starkbien of Sacramento, California, and Stanley Robert Humphrey of Hillsboro, Oregon.

Percy's father was the first minister of the Oakridge Open Bible Standard Church.

William H. Jenkins

William Jenkins, born May 15, 1911, and Josephine Stiffy, born June 10, 1916, were married in 1936. They lived in Oakridge from 1947 to 1969. They had one son, William Gregory "Greg" Jenkins.

Josephine "Jo" was a beauty operator and she and Bill owned the dry cleaners that was on First Street. They were both active in Boy Scouts, Lions Club and Methodist Church. Jo was a member of Business and Professional Women.

Greg Jenkins married Sondra Whitaker. They both went to school in Oakridge. They have two children, Tracy Lynn and John Gregory Jenkins.

William "Bill" died in August of 1987. Jo lives in Gig Harbor, Washington, and Greg lives in Anchorage, Alaska.

Dean E. Jowers

Dean Jowers, born October 21, 1918, and Shirley Tracy, born July 22, 1927, were married in 1948. Dean moved to Westfir in 1946 and worked for Hines Lumber Company. Shirley and Dean have one son, Dean Tracy Jowers.

Shirley graduated from Oakridge High School in 1944, attended business school, then worked for Hines Lumber Company in the sales office and also worked at Oakridge Clinic from 1951 to 1956.

Shirley worked at Croner's Drug Store and Uptown Theatre during her high school years and at Silver's (Henry Stein's) Confectionery after graduation.

When Dean lived in the area he was a car loader, shipping clerk and greenchain foreman at Hines. He also worked for Val Lee and Jim Hill in their service stations.

Shirley said, "When we lived in Oakridge, all the streets were dirt, the only sidewalks were board and the kids swam in the river. The road to Salmon Creek Falls was a one-lane road, the highway to Eugene was gravel until you got to Dexter. Highway 58 was under construction, the tunnel was not yet complete."

Gordon Julian

Phyllis L. McMahon and Gordon Julian were married in 1952. Gordon, a professor of biochemistry at Harvard Medical School and later at Montana State University, met Phyllis in Eugene, Oregon. Phyllis worked for Darling, Vonderheit and Morse (Wayne Morse's law firm). When they lived in Montana, Phyllis worked for the Montana State Fish and Game Department.

Gordon and Phyllis have two daughters, Nancy Louise (born 1953) and Janet Marie (born 1954).

Phyllis moved back to Oregon in 1979 and back to Oakridge in 1986. She has been active in civic affairs. She is a member of the City Planning Commission, Chairman of the Tree Planting Festival, and she organized the Fabulous Forties anniversary party and reunion. She has worked in movies and television as well as on the stage.

Frank Howard Klein

Frank Klein, born September 3, 1912, in White Salmon, Washington, married Eva Mae Winkelman. She was born April 26, 1914. She lived with her family in Oakridge after 1928. Her father Virgil Winkelman was a foreman on the railroad. Her brothers were Virgil, Jr., and William (Harry) and her sister was Iva. Her mother was Hattie.

Frank and Eva Klein operated a theater in Oakridge from 1946 to 1953. Frank lived in the area from 1932 to 1952.

Roy L. Knapp

Roy L. Knapp, born 1906, married Opal Sears in 1927 and moved to Oakridge in 1939. They had one son, Roy P. Knapp. Roy worked for Western Lumber Company and for Edward Hines Lumber Company at Westfir. He worked on the logging railroad for 14 years and in the machine shop for 18 years. He retired from Hines in 1971.

Emery Seymore LaDuke

Emery LaDuke married Mary Jane "Kate" Blunk. They came from Elizabeth, Indiana, to Oregon and settled on the Upper Willamette in 1900. They brought four children with them and had one more child, born in Lane County.

Their children were Otto "Spot" (born 1892), Emory (born 1884), Sarah Victoria (born 1889), Chilton L. (born 1899), Archie E. (born 1903) and Andrew "Punch" (born 1907).

Many descendants of Emery and Kate live in the Upper Willamette area.

Don LaDuke is the son of Otto; Bud LaDuke is the son of Archie; Pat and Michael are sons of Bud LaDuke. There are many others not listed here.

There were three LaDuke men listed in the 1933 roster of the Oakridge C.C.C. Company 943. They were A. LaDuke, C. LaDuke and O. LaDuke.

William K. LaMar

William LaMar, born February 22, 1909, at Eckert, Colorado, and Gertrude Shedd, born April 26, 1916, were married in 1957 and moved to Oakridge in 1958. Bill worked as a saw filer at Pope & Talbot.

George W. Larison

George W. Larison married Stella Pengra in 1866. She was the daughter of Bynon J. Pengra of Springfield. George was one of the first loggers in the Upper Willamette area. He drove logs down the river to the Pengra mill at Springfield. Larison Creek and Larison Rock are named for George.

George and Stella lived in a small cabin built on the bench at the site of the east portal of the present railroad tunnel. Their home was the first home on the present site of Oakridge. It was built on the Pengra land grant. All of the present city of Oakridge was at one time either the Pengra land grant or the Sanford ranch.

Their child, born in 1867, was the first white child born on Big Prairie.

When David Kitson built a large house on the Pengra land grant for Bynon J. Pengra, rock for the fireplace and lumber for the house were hauled by George

Larison who used his logging teams for the job. The large Pengra house was later occupied by Ella Pengra Walker and James A. Walker. Ella and Stella were sisters.

Virgil Leaming

Virgil Leaming, born September 3, 1925, at York, Nebraska, and Margaret Baylis, born February 23, 1927, at Portland, Oregon, were married January 14, 1949. They bought the Oak Market and moved to Oakridge in January 1963. The store was on the west side of the Oak Shopping Center. The Leamings had 12 employees and the store was open 7 days a week. They sold the store in 1978. Part of the shopping center burned down and after that a big new store was built and the shopping center was renamed Mountain View.

Virgil and Margaret took a two-year vacation from store ownership and did some traveling. Then in 1980 they bought the Oakridge Builders Supply and called it Virg's Builders Supply. They operated that business until August 1988 when they sold it. They are again free to travel and see new places.

Margaret and Virgil have one son Robert Leaming who married Terry Martin and they had two children, Robert William (Will) and Cortnee Doreen Leaming. Margaret and Virgil continue to make their home in Oakridge.

Paul Lyda

Paul Lyda, born April 27, 1926, in Kuna, Idaho, married Grace Kellom, born July 12, 1926. They married in 1944 and moved to Westfir in 1953. He worked for Edward Hines Lumber Company and they left the area in 1979. Their son Terry Lyda married Mary Dean, the daughter of Vicki and Alvin Dean. Both young people grew up in the Westfir-Oakridge area. Terry is a millworker and Mary is a homemaker. Mary and Terry have two children, Heidi and Talana Lyda.

Dan Lynch

Dan Lynch, born May 18, 1920, in Derby, Kansas, came to Oakridge in 1939 to work at the C.C.C. camp. The first day on the job, he helped install a water line to Blue Pool campground. He later worked in the mess hall becoming cook by the end of his stay.

June 28, 1940, Dan married Betty Oleson of Oakridge. They went to Medford in 1942 where Dan cooked for Morrison Knudsen who were building Camp White. They returned to Oakridge and Dan went to work for Southern Pacific until 1955. After that, he did a lot of building and worked for both Hines and Pope & Talbot. He was a millwright at Pope & Talbot when he retired on disability in 1973.

In 1944 and 1945, Dan served in the Medical Detachment of the 32nd Division, U.S. Army.

Betty and Dan have a son and daughter, Dee (born 1943) and Anna Marie (born 1946). Both attended school in Oakridge.

While in the C.C.C., Dan cooked on the Chetco fire and for the side camp at Waldo Lake while they were building the campgrounds.

Oscar Benedict McAtee

Oscar Benedict McAtee, born 1885, married Margaret Lena Knoop. He owned and operated a grocery store in Oakridge from 1923 until it burned in 1935. He then built a store, a garage, cabins and a bowling alley in Willamette City. He came to Oakridge from Kansas in 1923. His wife Margaret was born in 1888. They had six children — Hazel M. (Tiller, born 1911), Mildred M. (Allen, born 1914), Minnie E. (Robertson, born 1916), LeRoy G. (born 1919), Norris N. (born 1923) and Mary Jane (Carlino, born 1927).

The McClane Family

Thomas McClane was born in 1828 in Pennsylvania. In 1862, he married Harriet Wilcox who was born in 1842 in Illinois.

In 1863, they crossed the plains to California with four other families, the Addison Blacks, W.P. Allens, W. Woods and Charles Mathenys. After eight years in California, the families all moved to Oregon and settled at Big Prairie in 1871. Allen, Woods and Matheny took homesteads on High Prairie. Black took one where the Pope & Talbot mill pond was located, and McClanes took one between what was to be Westfir and Oakridge. The youngest McClane child, John, was born after they came to Big Prairie.

The McClane children were: Almanza C. (born 1863, died 1947 at Oakridge, never married), Charles E. (born 1864, died 1943 at Oakridge, never married), Mary (born 1866, died 1915, married Baxter Young), Anna May (born 1868, died 1945, married Volney Robinett, was first Hazeldell postmistress in 1880's), Mark (born 1870, died 1958, married Ivy Castleman) and John (born at Big Prairie in 1880, married Grace Bailey).

The oldest son, Almanza (Allie) bought the homesteads of Charlie Tufti and Jim Chuck Chuck. These properties were later sold to the Dunning and Holt families.

The youngest son, John, lived on the old family homestead until recently when poor health forced them to move to Dexter.

John and his wife Grace had two children, John Harold (born 1922) and Geneva (born 1925). Their son John Harold McClane died at Oakridge in 1950. Geneva is now Mrs. Wayne Boeckman.

Carol Ann McFarland, J.D.

Carol A. McFarland was born August 25, 1951. She is an attorney. Her children are Annette C. Miller-McFarland and Miles P. Miller-McFarland.

Corley Byrl McFarland

Corley Byrl McFarland, born 1886 in Iowa, came to Oakridge in 1924. He worked for the United State Forest Service, ranger, Boy Scout chairman, school board member and church board member. He married Ruth Hyland in 1918. She was born in Lowell, Oregon, in 1896 and attended the University of Oregon. They had two sons, Lee Lowery and Harvey John. C.B. McFarland died at his home in June 1969. Ruth Hyland McFarland died in November 1973.

Harvey John McFarland

Harvey John McFarland, born July 21, 1925, in Eugene, Oregon, married Muriel Walker on June 12, 1948. Muriel was born May 9, 1927; she is a teacher and homemaker. Harvey is an engineer and road building contractor. He graduated from Oregon State University, Corvallis, Oregon, in 1951. Prior to that, he served in the Air Force and upon returning from the service he worked as a topographer for the Forest Service. They mapped the Salmon Creek drainage above Oakridge. That was to work for Rosboro Lumber Company as their logging engineer. He worked for Rosboro until 1967. In that year, he formed Sur-Mac Construction, Inc. He was in that business from 1967 to 1987. They built several large projects and opened up areas for logging. Some of those areas were where he had ridden horseback with his father, C.B. McFarland in 1930 and 1931, just prior to the start of the C.C.C. development era.

Harvey and Muriel have five children — Mark, Carol, Jean, Beth and Robin.

Lee L. McFarland

Lee McFarland, born May 22, 1930, and his wife Sally have four children — Kirk L., Bonny Sue, Jenny Lee and Heather Ann.

Lee is the youngest son of C.B. McFarland, long-time Forest Ranger and resident on McFarland Road. His mother was Ruth Hyland McFarland. Her father owned the Oakridge Hotel in 1909. Lee grew up in Oakridge and spent summers working for the U.S.F.S. while going to school.

Mark L. McFarland, D.V.M.

Mark L. McFarland, born June 7, 1950, married Joan Townes. Joan was born October 31, 1950. They have three children — Corley Wm., Emily A. and Chad L.

William James McGillvrey

William James McGillvrey was born at Hawarden, Iowa, in 1900 and came to Oakridge in 1924 to work on railroad construction. He cut timber for the railroad right of way. Later he worked as a timber faller for lumber firms. July 1, 1925, he married Anna Lindsay who was born 1908 at Grants Pass, Oregon. The couple have made Oakridge their home since 1925 and they are the parents of three children — James McGillvery, Ernest McGillvrey and Ellen McGillvrey (Skidmore).

Donald Harvey McMahon

Donald H. McMahon, born 1931 in Westfir, Oregon, married Edna M. Strakbein on March 8, 1952. He died in a logging accident in May of 1955. They had two children — Linda Kay (born August 18, 1953) and William D. (born October 19, 1954).

William Arthur McMahon, Sr.

William A. McMahon, Sr., born 1890 in Fall Creek, Oregon, and Ferril Amanda Cain, born Landax area in 1898, were married in Eugene on December 24, 1917. They came to Westfir in 1925 and he worked for Western Lumber Company and its successors until 1955. William died in 1959.

Their children were Evelyn M. (born 1919), William A., Jr. (born 1920), Phyllis L. (born 1928) and Donald H. (born 1931).

William, Sr., trapped and hunted in the 1920's and 30's. For a time, he ran the loading operation at the old incline, where logs cut on High Prairie were yarded down to the North Fork by cable and hauled to the mill. Ferril and William gardened and farmed. They lived for many years in a house that sat between McLane Creek and Westoak Road. They had 90 acres on the hill across the road.

William Arthur McMahon, Jr.

William A. McMahon, Jr., born November 20, 1920, in Lowell, Oregon, married Bobbie Sorensen on May 20, 1945. Bobbie was born August 3, 1923. William was a logger for Hines Lumber Co. before and after serving in the U.S. Navy. He died in 1972.

Bobbie was business manager for Oakridge Clinic for seven years, business manager for Oakridge Insurance for eight years and self employed the rest of the time. Bobbie's parents were Bill and Ina Sorensen.

William and Bobbie had one daughter, Susan K. McMahon, who was born December 31, 1955, and died October 3, 1986. Susan had two children, Ryan J. Gonet (born July 9, 1977) and Joseph Wm. Penasso (born June 17, 1985).

William Dean McMahon

William D. McMahon, born October 19, 1954, married Lori Tomlin on March 2, 1975. Lori was born August 30, 1957. William (Bill) has worked for Pope & Talbot since 1976. They have four children — Jacob, Shelby, Kyle and Brittney Ferral.

Samuel P. Montgomery

Samuel P. Montgomery, born 1903 at Mead, Oklahoma, married Lillie Schiewe, born 1902, at Mulino, Oregon. They moved to the area in 1933. They had three children — Darrell, Lowell and Lynette. Lillie had been a legal secretary and a school teacher. After moving to Westfir, she was a homemaker and substitute teacher. She was active in the Westfir Community Church.

Sam worked on Highway 58 and then for the mill at Westfir under three ownerships. He also worked as a custodian and bus driver for Westfir School District. Later he was a truck driver and mechanic for Hines Lumber Company. Lillie and Sam still live in Westfir.

Rollo J. Morris

Rollo J. Morris, born November 27, 1919, in Longeaton, England, and Blanche Gastawbide, born April 8, 1924, were married in 1946. They moved to Oakridge in 1949. Rollo worked in the schools as a teacher, principal and librarian.

Rollo and Blanche had two boys, John R. and George A. Morris. They both went to school in Oakridge and both graduated from O.S.U. George continued into Law School and is now practicing in Eugene. John works in children's rehab in Denver. George and his wife Pam have two children, Joe and Kevin.

The Morris family lived in Oakridge for 35 years.

Clyde Parker Mount

Clyde Mount, born 1914, at Oregon City, Oregon, married Fumiko Ezawa, born September 10, 1925, at Chibaken, Japan. They moved to Oakridge in 1957 where Clyde was employed by Pope & Talbot until he retired in 1977. He died in 1983.

Fumiko spoke little English when she came to Oakridge, but she went to work at Midway Gardens and worked there for 20 years learning English as she worked.

The Mounts built a home on Fairy Glen Drive. They had two children, Robert Ezawa Mount and Momikai Ezawa Mount. Both children were born in Japan. Robert Mount is in the U.S. Air Force. Momikai Mount married Robert A. Dean.

Fumiko sold the family home in Oakridge and moved to Bend in 1985.

Chester C. Naro

Chester C. Naro, born in 1928 in Seattle, Washington, married Mapril Large, born in 1932. They moved to Oakridge in 1958 where they owned and managed Ridgeway Rollerdome. Chester died in 1979. Chester (Chet) and Mapril taught skating and their students brought home many medals in regional contests. For instance, at the Winter 1971 Northwest Regional Inter-Club Skating Championships, they brought home 21 medals from a possible 35. Winning students at that time were: Lisa Henry, Dale Naro, Judy Pflughaupt, Denise Clark, Andy Clark, Jannel Skoubo, Darrell Naro, Debbie Hills, Don Bailey, Patti Torgeson, Curtis Cline, Deanna Frederickson, Sharon Follet, Janet Kingrey, Betsy Trentz, Laurie Johnson, Nanette Gilbert, Rae Elliott, Brad Lundberg, Scott Johnson, Kathy Skoubo and Shane Henry. The championships were held at Vancouver, Washington.

David C. Naro

David C. Naro, born 1949, married Cherie A. Doppee, born 1947. They were married in 1973. Their children are David N. (born 1974), Derek (born 1976), Ronald (born 1965) and Veronica D. (born 1987).

Dale A. Naro

Dale A. Naro, born 1950, married Debbie Perkins, born 1955. They have three children, Dacia (born 1980), Dane (born 1986) and Danae (born 1988).

Darrell T. Naro

Darrell T. Naro, born 1956, married Judy Pflughaupt, born 1957. They have one child Dezerae J. born in 1981.

Ole Neet

Ole Neet, born 1871 in Kansas, married Sadie Troth and lived in the Lowell-Fall Creek area. He was a logger and a musician. They were the parents of ten children — Daisy Petit of Fall Creek; Vida Walsh of Springfield; Anna Lawson of Springfield; Ida Fox of Garberville, California; Viola James of Pleasant Hill; Art Neet of Fall Creek; Margaret Carter of Springfield; Ancil Neet of Fall Creek; Esther Neet of Oroville, California; and Warren Neet of Roseburg, Oregon. Ole was a son of Rachel and Joseph Neet of Fall Creek.

Vernon M. Neet

Vernon Neet, born January 31, 1913, at Myrtle Creek, Oregon, lived in Oakridge from 1936 to 1955. He worked for Southern Pacific Railroad Co. He and his wife Dorothy were married in 1939.

Gilbert Nelson

Gilbert Nelson was born in 1889 and his wife Myrtle was born in 1891. They moved from California to Westfir in 1927. Gilbert was head sawyer for Westfir Lumber Co. and Myrtle was a homemaker. Leon "Tyke" Nelson is their son.

Leon "Tyke" Nelson

Leon Nelson, born July 22, 1916, at LaGrande, Oregon, and Cleo Kearns, born May 23, 1918, were married at the Oakridge Methodist Church in 1937.

They had two children, Michael (born 1938) and Maureen (born 1942). Michael went to school in Westfir and Oakridge. He married Jeri Pickens and they have three children, David, Tina and John. Maureen married Ted Keller and had two children, Scott and Dan.

"Tyke" worked for Westfir Lumber Company after graduating from high school. He went to work for the schools in 1947 and worked as a custodian and bus driver until 1977. Cleo Nelson died in 1977. As of 1989, "Tyke" has lived 63 years in the Upper Willamette.

Francis Wm. "Bill" Niemi

Bill Niemi, born 1923, at Taft, Oregon, and Helena Ruth Bones, born 1924, were married in 1942 at Turner, Oregon. Bill was in the U.S. Air Force for eight years during World War Two and the Korean Conflict. He came to Oakridge in September of 1953 to work for Hills Chevrolet as a mechanic. He continued to work at the garage under other owners including Cowart, Burton and Bolin.

Bill served as President of Lions Club and P.T.A., as chairman of Oakridge Park Board and on many committees at the Methodist Church. He promoted the development of Osprey and Salmon Creek Parks in the city.

Ruth was President of Volunteer Service Council (1968–1971), Oakridge Anti-Poverty Program Coordinator (1972–1979) and was on the Lane County Extension Advisory Council. In 1986, Ruth was selected to be a hostess in the Oregon Pavilion at the 1986 Expo in Vancouver, B.C., Canada.

Bill and Ruth had six children — Wilma Pauline (Paula), Harold A., William M., George H., Roger D. and Melvin E. Niemi.

Paula married Dennis Anderson, the son of Buford Anderson. George married Sheryl Batson of Oakridge. Melvin married Janice Splawn.

Bill Niemi died in 1984.

Alvin C. Noland

Alvin C. Noland, born September 23, 1930, married Peggy Norris and they had three children — Donald L., Daniel A. and Gloria D. (Harp). They all went to school in Westfir and Oakridge.

Alvin lived in Westfir from 1930 to 1958. Alvin was a plannerman for Edward Hines Lumber Company. He and Peggy divorced in 1972. In 1982, Alvin married Doris J. Swanson and they live in Eugene.

Daniel and Melonie Noland have two sons, Ian and Isaac.

Cleveland Noland

Cleveland and his wife Mary Jane lived in Westfir in the early days of railroad logging on the North Fork. He was an engineer on the railroad. He was engineer on the first and last trips that the logging train made.

Cleveland and Mary Jane had three children, Helen M. (Harris), Alvin C. and Elmer D. Noland. They all went to school in the area.

John O'Connell

John and Franchon O'Connell and their sons, Tom and Larry, moved to Oakridge in 1937. They made the trip from Iowa in a 1928 Chevrolet. Their son Bob had come to Oakridge in 1936. Their daughter Eileen came later in 1937.

Three of the children graduated from Oakridge High School — Eileen in 1938, Tom in 1941 and Larry in 1947.

John and each of the children worked at one time for Southern Pacific. John became assistant section foreman in Oakridge. He retired in 1957 at age 70.

John and Franchon helped to get St. Michael's Catholic Church built.

Their son Bob became an engineer on the railroad. Larry became a teacher, Eileen retired from BLM and Tom retired from Southern Pacific.

Like pioneers of earlier times, the O'Connells came west and made a new life for themselves on the Upper Willamette. They were a part of the Depression Era migration when many made the trip from all parts of the Midwest.

LeRoy Oleson, Sr.

LeRoy Oleson was born June 4, 1897, in Cohasset, Minnesota. He came to Oregon in 1903. He joined the Army when he was 14 years old and was sergeant by the time he was 18 years old. He was stationed at Old Fort Lewis, Washington. He met his wife while he was there.

Judith Nordgren and LeRoy were married May 21, 1921. They had seven children — Betty (born 1922), Tom (born 1923), Lindy (born 1927), Annie (born 1929), Katy (born 1932), Mildred (born 1934) and LeRoy, Jr. (born 1938).

LeRoy went to work for Southern Pacific in 1922 and lived at many of the railroad locations, Natron, Pryor, the railhead seven miles above Oakridge (1925) and Oakridge. In 1932, they moved to a house on Salmon Creek Road.

LeRoy was a section foreman for the railroad. He retired in 1965 after 43 years working for Southern Pacific. He died in 1973. His widow Judith celebrated her 87th birthday at a family reunion at Greenwaters Park in 1989. About 80 family members attended.

Thomas Orr

Thomas Orr and his wife Lucinda Sanford Orr came to Oregon by way of Cape Horn in 1857. Their one-year-old daughter Theresa was with them. In 1858, they were at Eugene City when a son, Richmond, was born. Mrs. Eugene Skinner took care of the mother and new baby. After a brief stay in Oregon, the family returned to Illinois where four more children were born before they came again to Oregon. Thomas died in Illinois and Lucinda brought her children west and took a place near her brother, James Sanford, in Hazeldell(see *Biographical Sketches, Israel Gray*).

Lawrence Wesley Owens

L. "Wes" Owens was born February 2, 1928, at Spavinaw, Oklahoma. He came with his family to Oregon, received a Master's Degree from Linfield College in 1953. He began teaching at Oakridge High School in 1954.

In 1969, he married home economics teacher Carla Mae Vaughn. They had two children, Wesley Blaine and Monica Leigh Owens.

Wes was honored in 1981 by the Oregon State Coaches and was selected to coach the AAA all-star team. He coached at the high school and for the Upper Willamette Youth Association.

He retired from teaching in 1983 and took a number of part-time jobs. He worked for B.L.M., Willamette Pass Corp. and the Oregon State Highway Department. He died in 1988 while working on a Highway 58 construction project. His death was the result of an accident. Wes was a loved and respected teacher, coach and family man.

Charles A. Paddock

Charles Paddock, born in 1897 in Schenectady, New York, first came to Oakridge in 1909 as a trapper. He then returned to New York and married Ella Beulah Worden, born 1893 in Balston Spa, New York. Charles A., Jr. and Pearl J. were born there.

Charles, Beulah and family came to Oakridge to stay in 1919. Charles built a number of houses and the Uptown Market. He ran the market for several years. He organized a Boy Scout troop and was the first City Recorder. He was a union organizer and active in politics. He built Midway Gardens Florists and greenhouses and was active in that business with Beulah, son Ronel and daughter-in-law Lynette.

Son Ronel was born in 1927 after the family came to Oakridge. Charles died in 1970 and Beulah in 1982. She continued to work in the greenhouse until about 1978.

James Paddock

In 1924, James and Winifred Paddock of Ballston Spa, New York, decided to go west and make their home in Oakridge, Oregon. James had a brother, Charles Paddock, who had already come to Oregon, and since James and Charles had married sisters, Winifred's sister Beulah was also out west.

The trip west was made with two trucks, the family driving from New York to Oakridge. They arrived in June of 1924. With them were their five children who had been born in New York.

As soon as they found living quarters, James started building a building to house a hardware store. He owned and operated this enterprise for 25 years.

James and his brother Charles worked hard to obtain the incorporation of the City of Oakridge, and James served as the first mayor. James also served as a director for the Lane County Electric Cooperative.

After the family came to Oakridge, a sixth child was born. He was named James Paddock, Jr. He went to school in Oakridge and has been maintenance and operations superintendent for Lane County Electric Cooperative out of the Eugene office. He has a wife, Evelyn, and two sons, Jamie and Gordon.

The other children of James and Winifred are Olive (Mrs. Howard) Bernhart of Beaverton, Oregon; Worden Paddock of Dayton, Oregon; Etta (Mrs. Virgil) Herndon of Lincoln City, Oregon; Eleanor (Mrs. Osburn) Fisher of Springfield, Oregon and June (Mrs. Ernest) Poggie of San Francisco, California.

James and Winifred died at Oakridge and are buried at the Forestvale Cemetery.

Ronel M. Paddock

Ronel Paddock, born November 14, 1927, in Oakridge, Oregon, married Lynette Montgomery of Westfir on July 23, 1950. They have two children, Charles B. Paddock (born 1952) and Sandra M. Paddock (born 1957).

Ronel and Lynette assumed the business of Midway Gardens from his parents in 1952 and continued to operate the business. Ron has been active in community organizations as an officer in Chamber of Commerce, United Methodist Church, Lane County Democratic Central Committee (youngest chairman ever) 1955–1958, State of Oregon Democratic Executive Board, Oakridge-Westfir Jay-Cees, Oakridge City Council, Countryside Beautification Committee 1966–1971, Lane Council of Governments, League of Oregon Cities, Forestvale Cemetery Association, Oakridge Pioneer

Museum Association and Mayor of Oakridge 1970–1978. He serves and has served as chairman or president of most of the organizations.

Lynette has been active in the business and has been active in Lane County and Oakridge Democratic Women and Lane County Democratic Central Committee. Charter member Upper Willamette Business and Professional Women and member United Methodist Church.

Their son Charles married Diane Waddle of Westfir. They have two children, Carrie Lynn and Charles Mathew. Charles works for Multnomah County and Diane is an R.N. working at Meridian Park Hospital.

Sandra M. Paddock married Francis Pokorny in 1978. Francis served in Vietnam and works for the U.S. Forest Service as a core driller. Sandra is a homemaker. They have two children, Charles Anthony and Olivia P.

Joe C. Priddy

Joe C. Priddy, born 1921, married Elaine Young, born 1922. They lived in Oakridge from 1948 to 1955 and started Zephyr Cleaners at First and Beach Streets. They were charter members of the Chamber of Commerce and Lions Club.

The polio vaccine was discovered at that time. Elaine Priddy went from house to house in the area convincing parents to have their children vaccinated. There were a few who did not. Then when Ruth Clark, who was popular and well known in the community, got polio, most agreed to have the life-saving vaccine. (See *Biographical Sketches, Earl Clark*).

Elaine and Joe have three children — Rebecca, Mark and Bruce.

Jay S. Putnam

Jay S. Putnam was born in Bakersfield, California, on October 20, 1917. He moved to Oakridge in 1928, graduated from Oakridge High School, attended Willamette University and University of Oregon and then was in the Army for four-and-one-half years. He married Jeanne Lindsay in 1942. Jeanne and Jay had three daughters, Carol, Janet and Catherine. Jeanne died in 1961.

Jay and Alice Salsbury of Laurel, Montana, were married in November of 1964. Alice moved to Oakridge.

Alice Salsbury Putnam, born in Winnipeg, Manitoba, Canada, on October 23, 1919, attended the University of Manitoba and graduated from Winnipeg Teachers College. She was teacher and principal. She married Arthur H. Salsbury, horticulturist, in 1944. They lived in Montana and had two daughters, Gayle and Donna. Arthur died in a plane crash in 1960.

When Alice moved to Oakridge, her daughter Gayle Salsbury and Jay's daughter Carol Putnam were in college. Donna Salsbury and the Putnam girls graduated from Oakridge High School. Catherine Putnam was the first "Future First Citizen of the Year" for Oakridge.

In 1949, Jay had purchased the E.E. Smith General Store, one of the original stores in the area. In 1957, he went to work for Pope & Talbot and was particle board plant foreman. He worked as accountant/manager for the Chevrolet dealership from 1961 to 1980. Since then, he has been a tax consultant.

Jay has served the community in many ways — on the school board, on the school and city budget committees, the Tree Planting Association and as a member of the Chamber of Commerce. Jay served in many capacities in the United Methodist Church.

After moving to Oakridge in 1964, Alice was kept busy with work for her home, church and community. She was chosen "Citizen of the Year" for 1988. She has served on the Oakridge City Council (1980 to 1984), member of election board for ten years, served on the United Methodist Church administrative council and was a certified lay speaker. She tutored physically handicapped children, served as an officer for Lane County Home Extension, Garden Club, Chamber of Commerce and other organizations. She is a member of O.E.S. and P.E.O. She was named Lane County Senior Woman of the Year in 1981. She does free tax service for low-income people.

Jay and Alice have been members of the Methodist choir. Jay plays piano and organ and Alice is a soloist and in years past sang with "The Five of Us," a local singing group under the direction of Ercle Ramey. The group sang for functions all over the state.

Since being semi-retired, Jay and Alice enjoy spending vacations in Arizona where they promote Oakridge and the Upper Willamette area.

Roy Putnam

Roy was roadmaster for Southern Pacific Railroad for a district roughly from Lowell to Cascade Summit. He and his family lived in Oakridge from 1928 to 1938.

His son Jay recalled coming to Oakridge on the old military road in a 1925 Essex driven by his mother Irene. They spent their first night in Oakridge at the Woods Hotel.

William J. Rardin

William J. Rardin, born 1899 in Oakland, Oregon, came to Oakridge in 1923. He worked on the building of the railroad and in the woods. He and his wife Hortense Sheffield, born 1897 in Utah, were members of the Open Bible Standard Church. Their children were N. James, Charlotte (McKinnis), Thomas (Jack), Ruth (Churan), Billie (Hatfield), Ella M. (Jones) and Helen (Parks).

Ralph Clinton Ream

Ralph Clinton Ream married Joanna F. Dunning in 1942. They make their home on McFarland Road near Oakridge and are the parents of Michael Ralph Ream and Terry Joe Ream.

Russel Reed

Russel Reed, born 1944, married Janice Tomlin, born 1947. They have three children — Mika Suzanne, Jeffrey and Russel. Janice lived in Oakridge all her life. Russel worked for Pope & Talbot.

Edgar (Eddie) N. Roberts

Edgar N. Roberts, born June 15, 1924, and F. Dolores Pettijohn, born January 7, 1925, were married in 1956.

Eddie is a contractor. He has lived all his life in Oakridge where his father proved up on a homestead. His brother James lives on the home place east of Oakridge.

The Roberts children are:

Charles O. Roberts married Genie Spenser and they have two children, Peter and Staci.

Terry M. Roberts married Rosalie Zaln and they have two children, Kari and Thomas.

John E. Roberts married Rebecca Wright and they have four children, James, Steward, Michael and Chad.

Larry D. Roberts married Debra Miller and they have a daughter Kate.

Carol J. Roberts married Warren Tripp and they have two children, Kristopher and Diane.

William D. Roberts married Patti Bergman Denny and they have four children, Dustin and Lyndi Roberts and Julie and Michael Denny.

Gerald G. Roberts married Cherri Kloster and they have two children, Nathan and Amanda.

Christy D. Roberts married Robin Truelove and they have two children, Valarie and Kelli.

All of the Roberts children went to Oakridge schools all or part of the time.

Edgar's father was James E. Roberts and his mother was Bessie Neyman Roberts. His brother is James H. Roberts.

Charles Lee Rockwell

Charles Rockwell, born September 19, 1913, came to Westfir in 1939. Audrey Haskett Rockwell came to Westfir with her parents, Thomas and Marie Haskett, in 1943. Audrey was born February 20, 1927. She worked in the Westfir Lumber Company cookhouse while going to high school at Oakridge.

Charles and Audrey had three children, Charles, Jr., Marjorie and Erik.

Charles worked on the pond at the Westfir mill for 35 years. He was a lead man and barker operator.

Audrey was a recreation director at Westfir for 13 years. She was a custodian at Westfir and Oakridge Schools for 13 years. She was elected Mayor of Westfir and took office in 1979 through 1984. She had done lots of volunteer work for Oakridge and Westfir.

Charles Rockwell, Jr. married Gay Butler and they have three children, Ryan, Todd and Tiffany.

Marjorie Rockwell married Mike Cross and they have four children, Mark, Mathew, Michelle and Charles Cross.

Erik Thomas Rockwell works at Lane Community College.

Luther E. Rogers

Luther Rogers, born June 6, 1896, and Inez Flock, born January 2, 1901, were married in 1919. Luther was a logger.

Inez and Luther had eight children — Oral, Calvin, Tharon (Kirby), Lyle, Arden, Cleone (Bain), Tracy and Tamaris (Clifford).

The Rogers were members of the United Methodist Church and Inez wrote articles for the Oakridge newspaper. She worked as a volunteer for Helping Hands for many years.

Luther died in 1981 and Inez died in 1985. Both are buried at Forestvale Memorial Park.

John Augustus Ryker

John Augustus Ryker was born in 1880 in Indiana and came to Oakridge in 1911. He drove freight wagons over the old Rigdon Road and later worked for the United States Forest Service. His wife was the former Manie D. Williams, born in 1880 in Tennessee. Gus and Manie were married in 1903.

They were the parents of eight children — Clarence A. Ryker, Lillian Ryker McGillvery, Edna Ryker Temple, Mamie Ryker Eskridge, Myrtis Ryker Wojcik, Louis S. Ryker, Edith Ryker Brown and Mary Ryker Pedigo.

Ben Ryman

Ben Ryman, born 1906, and Phyllis Sorensen, born 1913, were married in 1935. Ben was a sawfiler and Phyllis was Postmaster at Westfir from 1941 to 1949.

In 1965, Phyllis married James Brainard of Eugene. She moved back to Oakridge in 1986.

Josiah Sanford

Josiah Sanford, born 1801, lived in Richmond, Virginia, and came to Oregon with his sons, James and Richmond Sanford. They were the first settlers in Oakridge area. Josiah died in 1882 at Hazeldell (Oakridge) and was buried on the Sanford ranch and was later moved to the Pleasant Hill Cemetery where his sons and daughters are buried.

Richmond Sanford

Richmond Sanford, born in 1833 at Richmond, Virginia, was named for the city of his birth. He came to Oregon with his father, Josiah, and his brother, James. They were the first white settlers in the Oakridge area. Richmond was a cattleman. He had cattle at the Sanford ranch on the Upper Willamette and in eastern Oregon. Richmond died in eastern Oregon and was buried there. His remains were later moved to the Pleasant Hill Cemetery where other members of his family were buried.

Robert F. Sayre

Robert Sayre, born October 6, 1918, married Doris I. Walker, born August 19, 1921. Robert was a Southern Pacific Railroad engineer. He lived in Oakridge from 1933 to 1959. Doris lived in Oakridge from 1921 to 1959. She was the daughter of Grace and Earl Walker.

Robert and Doris had three children, Karen Lynn, Lacy H. and Michelle. Karen has two sons, Bret and Kyle Jones. Lacy married Colleen Evers. They have two sons, Mathew and Andru Sayre. Michelle married John Ayres. They have two daughters, Monica and Echo Ayres. Robert and Doris live in Eugene.

C. Avery Sherman

C. Avery Sherman married Mildred Flock in 1931. She was the daughter of James and Lina Flock of Oakridge. Mildred was born at Eugene, Oregon, in 1910. Avery and Mildred were the parents of four children — Francis Lamonte Sherman (born 1933), twin girls Beverly Jean Sherman (Stafford, born 1935) and Mildred Lenore Sherman (Vanderpool, born 1935), Louis Avery Sherman (born 1937). Both boys live in the Oakridge area and worked for Hines Lumber Company at Westfir. Avery Sherman died in 1948. In 1951, Mildred married George Chambers of eastern Oregon and he died in 1960.

Paul M. Sims

Paul M. Sims was born in 1906 in Yelleville, Arkansas. In 1928, he married Rose M. Mickley who was born in 1906 at Cape Horn, Washington. They came to the Oakridge area in 1940. He was stationed at Odell Lake Maintenance Station, first as assistant then as foreman for the State Highway Department, with responsibility for Highway 58 from Oakridge to Odell Butte.

Lack of educational facilities forced Paul to move the family to Oakridge in 1944 and soon after he resigned from the State Highway Department. In the years following this move, Paul worked as an independent mechanic, both in Oakridge and at Cresdell Lodge once located east of Crescent Lake Junction. In 1947-48, Paul operated a store and service station at McCredie Springs.

Rose was the last postmistress at the office located in the store, but continued working for the Postal Service until her retirement in 1965. Paul eventually returned to road maintenance, primarily with Pope & Talbot, until his retirement. Two children, Genevieve M. (Brewer, born 1930) and John P. (born 1931) are graduates of Oakridge High School, 1948 and 1949 respectively, and both now live in Oakridge. Paul died in 1980. Rose now lives with her daughter (See *Biographical Sketches, Robert Brewer* for the children and grandchildren of Genevieve).

Children and grandchildren of John P. Sims: Ann Marie (Bloom, born 1957, now of Eugene), Cathy L. (Lobben, born 1960, now of Kirkland, Washington) and Austin D. Lobben (born 1988).

William Sorensen

William "Bill" Sorensen came to Westfir in 1928 and moved his family there in 1931. His wife was Ina Ann Woodward Sorensen. Their children were Phyllis (Ryman, Brainard), Joseph, Marion, Margaret (McAtee, Long) and Barbara "Bobbie" (McMahon).

Bill was assistant plannerman at the Westfir mill from 1928 to 1956. Bill died in 1956 and Ina died in 1968.

Albert Spalinger

Albert Spalinger was born April 4, 1877, in Zurich, Switzerland. He came to Oregon while still an infant. He went to school in Oregon and became "head man" on a trolley car in 1899. Spalinger and Katherine Roth, born 1879 in Switzerland, were married in Portland, Oregon, on September 19, 1900.

In 1901, Spalinger went to work for Southern Pacific as a fireman and by 1907 he moved to the other side of the engine cab as an engineer. In 1927, he came to the Upper Willamette to work the engines from Oakridge to the Cascade Summit. The "helper" engines were put on in Oakridge to get the trains up over the mountains. They still use helper engines but they work out of Eugene now.

Albert and Katherine raised a family of six boys and one girl — Herman (born 1902), Edwin (born 1904), John (1905), Alvin (1910), Martin (Bim, born 1912), Katherine Elizabeth (Betty, born 1914) and Melvin (born 1918). Martin married Lois Walker and Betty married Donald Walker, Sr.

The Spalingers celebrated their golden anniversary in 1950.

Spalinger was forced to retire in 1941 because of a stroke. At the time of his retirement, he was running an engine that was a great contrast to the ones he first worked on. His last engine was a 4100 class Mallett with cab forward — one of the largest and most powerful made. He had operated wood burners, coal burners and oil burners, every type of engine in the Portland division. His early work was before such safety devices as automatic couplers, automatic block signalling and central dispatching systems. He put in 40 years of railroading. He died in 1956.

Albert Spalinger, Railroad Engineer

Katherine died in 1978, a year short of her hundredth birthday. She lived over 50 of those years in Oakridge raising her family and enjoying her friends.

Percy Stouky

Percy Stouky, born in Nevada in 1891, married Florence Holt in 1913. Florence was born in Iowa in 1897. Percy was a surveyor for the railroad through Oakridge. The family lived on Brock Road. Their children were Maxine (born 1914 in Mapleton, Oregon) and Betty (born 1916 in Oakridge, Oregon).

Louie Streit

Louie Streit was born November 9, 1898. He married Ella Tuchardt who was born September 8, 1896. They lived in Westfir from 1923 to 1947 and in Oakridge from 1947 to the late 1970's. He was dry kiln operator at the Westfir mill for 36 years. The Streits were instrumental in the formation of St. Michael Catholic Church in Oakridge.

They had three children — Robert, Richard and Helen. The children grew up and went to school in Westfir-Oakridge.

Richard W. Streit

Richard Streit, born November 19, 1925, in Westfir, Oregon, married Ruth Lovelady, born March 19, 1932. They married in 1950 and left Westfir in 1956. He worked at Hines Lumber Company.

Robert Streit

Robert Streit, oldest son of Ella and Louie Streit, graduated from Oakridge High School in 1940. He and his wife Carole had four children — Kellie (Murray), Scott, Salli (Smith) and Marla (Ciesiel). Robert died in 1989. They lived in Pendleton, Oregon.

Wilfred O. Svendsen

Wilford Svendsen, born November 6, 1909, at Hayfield, Minnesota, and Wilma Mays, born August 9, 1913, at Junction City, Oregon, were married April 20, 1935, in Eugene, Oregon. They had two sons, Richard A. and Charles W. Svendsen.

The family came to Oakridge in 1947 and opened a Marshall-Wells Hardware store in the Oddfellows Building. They were in partnership with Wilfred's father, Christian Svendsen. After ten years, the business was moved to the McAtee Building next to the bank. In 1959, Marshall-Wells sold to Coast-to-Coast Stores and the Svendsens became a franchised store with them. They had several employees over the years, but Beatrice Moisio was one who became "one of the family" and was with the store for many years.

Richard Svendsen married Nancy Ann Johnson in 1962 and they have two daughters, Cheryl Ann and Karen Lynn Svendsen.

Karen Lynn Svendsen married Jeffery Long and they have a son, Kyle Jeffery Svendsen Long.

Charles Svendsen and Susan Lennox were married in Oakridge on October 13, 1984. They have a daughter Lindsey Lennox and a son Brandon Lennox. Charles is a teacher in Oakridge.

Wilfred Svendsen died on July 8, 1984. Wilma married H. Harlan Boots on May 3, 1986.

Harry Swank

Harry Swank was born January 25, 1908, in Muncy Valley, Pennsylvania. In 1934, he married Evelyn Lindke, born May 12, 1918. They moved to Oakridge in 1947. Harry was Lane County Deputy Sheriff and Constable for the Upper Willamette District and Evelyn was a part-time police matron. Together they operated a small process serving business.

When Harry was Park Board Chairman for the city, Evelyn designed the gateway to Greenwaters Park and Harry and other volunteers built it. Harry worked on the Tree Planting Festival and was on the committee for the dedication of Hills Creek Dam.

Their children are Robert, Harry E., Elizabeth, Barbara and Jeanne.

Robert Swank and his wife Josephine had four children — Patricia, Cathy, Doris and Joanna. Harry E. Swank and his wife Christine have a son David. Elizabeth married Robert Edwards. Barbara married William Stellmacher and they have a son Isaac. Jeanne married Jeffrey Inmon.

Harry and Evelyn lived in Oakridge for 40 years. After Harry died, Evelyn moved to Eugene. None of their children stayed in the area.

Roy Temple

Roy Temple and Edna Ryker were married in 1925. Their only son, Don, was born December 9, 1930. Roy and Edna started the Willamette Pass Ski Area and operated it from 1941 to 1947. They owned and operated Temples Sporting goods in Oakridge until 1970. Roy was Oakridge Fire Chief from 1950 until 1957. Roy died in 1969 and Edna sold the store in 1970. Edna continued to be involved in community activities as a valuable volunteer.

Don Temple

Don Temple, born 1930, married Diane Dooley of Oakridge. They were the parents of Shirley and Greta Temple. Don died in 1969 as a result of a snowmobile accident. Don was an expert skier and a skiing companion of Jack Meissner, a popular instructor at Willamette Pass and other ski resorts.

Sherman William Tiller

Sherman William Tiller, born in Idaho in 1900, was a timber faller and owned and operated a bowling alley in Willamette City. In 1931, he married Hazel McAtee who was born in Kansas in 1911 and came to Oakridge in 1924. Their children were Dale Leroy, Verna May (Loudermilk), Wesley Ermal, Nadine Evelyn (Lunyou), Darlene Faye (Lister), Paul Allen, Patsy Joan (Gilliam), Donald Roy, Larry Gene and Nancy Marie.

Thomas Jefferson Tiller

Thomas Jefferson Tiller, born 1857 in Missouri, married Mary Ellen (Ella) Flock on December 22, 1891. She was born in 1867 in Indiana. Their children were Ermal Aaron (born 1894), Thurmon (born 1895), Sherman (born 1900), Jesse (born 1905), Hazel (born 1892), Rachel (born 1897) and Clara (born 1902).

Cris E. Tomlin

Cris E. Tomlin was born September 22, 1953. Cris is a millwright. He worked at Hines until it burned, then at Pope & Talbot. He married Betty Johnson. She has three children, Gary Vaughn, Kim Vaughn and Patric Scott Vaughn.

Gene Tomlin

Gene Tomlin, born March 8, 1930, in Greenbay, Wisconsin, married Audrey Koskey Randle in 1952. Gene lived in Oakridge since 1939, worked for Lane Electric Co-op for 22 years, owned Tall Cedars Trailer Court for 13 years and operates Mountain Valley Real Estate. His parents were N. Sam Tomlin and Louise Chambers Tomlin.

Audrey was born March 26, 1926. She married Donald Randle in 1945. They had two children, Janice and Mark. Randle died in 1950. Audrey married Gene Tomlin. They adopted her first two children and have two more children, Chris E. and Lori. Audrey's parents were Abel and Orpha Koskey. Abel worked for Hines Lumber Company and for Pope & Talbot. Orpha worked for almost every restaurant in the area, including operating one for George and Irene Thatcher in 1944.

Mark D. Tomlin

Mark D. Tomlin, born July 28, 1948, is an auto mechanic. He married Carol Torrence, a nurse. They have three children, Devon M., Deanna D. and Dwane. They have lived in the Lebanon area for the past ten years.

Robert E. Tracy, Sr.

Robert Tracy, born January 4, 1893, and Irene Reynolds, born October 19, 1903, were married in 1922. Irene and Robert had two children, Robert E., Jr., and Shirley B. Tracy (Jowers). They came from Portland to live in Oakridge in 1937. Robert was already working for Southern Pacific and was the fireman on the first freight train over the S.P. Cascade Line. He moved up to engineer in 1940. He retired in 1958 and continued to live in Oakridge until he died in 1970.

Irene worked part time at the Oakridge Post Office. She lived in Oakridge until 1972 and now lives with her daughter in Kirkland, Washington.

Robert E. Tracy, Jr., graduated from Oakridge High School in 1940, attended the University of Oregon and married Ellen Stillwell. They have two children, Shannon and Brad.

Shirley married Dean Jowers (see *Biographical Sketches, Jowers*).

Pauline (Freddie) Tullock, R.N.

Pauline Fredricksen was born October 5, 1915, at Cushing, Nebraska. She came to Westfir in 1939 and worked with Dr. George C. Varney from 1939 to 1942. She married Fredrick Michelsen in 1939. War was declared in 1941 and Fredrick joined the Navy in 1942 and died on active duty in 1945. Their son Fredrick John Michelsen was born August 6, 1945, at St. Paul, Nebraska. Freddie returned to Westfir and in December of 1946 she married Myron Budge Tullock who worked for Westfir Lumber Company and Hines Lumber Company until his retirement in 1977.

Freddie worked for Dr. Waldo E. Harris from 1948 to 1953 and was Westfir school nurse from 1953 to 1955. Her daughter Julie Myroene Tullock was born July 3, 1955. Freddie worked at Oakridge Clinic for a time and was Lane County Health nurse for Fall Creek, Lowell, Westfir, Oakridge and McCredie Springs from 1964 until she retired in 1977.

She was chosen Citizen of the Year for 1975.

Myron Budge Tullock died June 6, 1987.

E. Mildred Tveit

Evelyn Mildred McMahon, born 1919, married William F. West in 1935. They had two children, Patricia Ann and Robert Edward. Later she married Lavon Tveit and had another child, Carmen Lee.

Mildred has many interests. During World War Two, she worked at a mill in Sutherlin, Oregon. Later she worked as a chef in Florence, Oregon. She is a seamstress and tole painter and does other handwork.

Samuel Earl Walker

Samuel Earl Walker, born December 10, 1881, at Hazeldell (Oakridge), was born to Ella Pengra Walker and James A. Walker. He was a grandson of B.J. Pengra, Surveyor General of Oregon appointed by President Lincoln.

Earl's father died in 1896, so he and his brother had to quit school and go to work. They hired out cutting wood for Dave Kitson who owned Kitson Springs. They also did trapping, hunting and took care of the family farm.

Grace and Earl Walker on their 50th wedding anniversary on February 9, 1960.

Earl owned land that was at the west end of Oakridge and at one time was called Willamette City. He filed for homestead rights and proved up on it in 1916, 160 acres, the deed signed by Woodrow Wilson. A part of his land was subdivided and called Walker Addition. He had a sash and door plant and built several houses in that area.

He sold a right of way to Southern Pacific for $800 and he helped clear the land on the right of way.

In 1910, Earl married Grace Hills, the daughter of Jasper and Flora Neet Hills. They spent their honeymoon up the North Fork at Brock cabin. They did some trapping while they were there, coming home with lots of pelts.

Grace and Earl had three children, Donald Earl (born 1914), James Elwin (born 1918) and Doris Irene (born 1921). Their children all went to school in Oakridge.

The Walkers had a dairy farm in the 1920's and in 1932 they moved to High Prairie where they bought several ranches. In the 1950's, they built a house on a knoll near the Oakridge High School and moved back to town.

They were active in the United Methodist Church and in Oddfellows Lodge and Rebeccas. Earl helped build the Methodist Church. Earl was a man who could do many things — he built caskets when they were needed and he put stained glass in the church. He could farm or run a mill.

Grace and Earl spent 62 years together before she died in 1972. He died in 1977.

In his last years, the young people of the area called Earl "the old gentleman." That says a lot.

Two grandsons live in the area, Donald E. Walker, Jr., and Larry A. Walker.

James A. Walker

James Walker, born 1849 in Springfield, Missouri, died in 1896 at Hazeldell, Oregon. In 1877, he married Ella V. Pengra of Springfield, Oregon, who was born in 1855. She died at Oakridge in 1946. (See *Oregon Central Military Road* and *Bynon J. Pengra*).

James was a carpenter and he worked on the first bridge that was built at Springfield to cross the Willamette River. James and Ella had three children — William Sidney, Samuel Earl and Bessie Louise who married Roy Harvey.

William S. Walker

William S. Walker was born in 1878 at Springfield, Oregon, and came to Oakridge with his parents in 1880. He took a homestead on land now known as the Walker Addition of Oakridge. His father died when he was a boy causing him and his brother to start working while they were quite young. William was a farmer and a carpenter who had a reputation for being a good neighbor. He also served on the school board.

In 1903, William married Olive May Gray, the daughter of Israel and Theresa Gray of Oakridge (then Hazeldell). Olive Gray was born in 1881 at Onarga, Illinois, and came to the Upper Willamette area in 1882. Olive went to school at the Hazeldell school. William and Olive had four children — Louise E. (born 1904, married Ed Clark), Wayne V. (born 1905, married Thelma Carter), Elsie G. (born 1910 and married Winston Allard, a professor of journalism who died in 1953) and Lois W. (born 1914, married Martin Spalinger).

Frank Warner

Frank Warner was born at Fall Creek. His parents were Fred and Elizabeth Warner who came to Oregon with the "Lost Wagon Train" of 1853. Frank married Susan Emaline Neet who was born in Iowa and came to Oregon when she was 18 years old. Frank and Susan bought the Black place, probably about 1880. Mr. Black had a post office at his place from 1873 until 1879, so we know he was still on the place at that time.

Frank and Susan were the parents of four girls — Elizabeth Warner (McDowell, born 1884, died 1926), Lina Warner (Flock, born 1886, died 1956), Isabelle Warner (Abrams, born 1888) and Flora Warner (Dompier, born 1896, died 1949).

Fred Warner

Fred Warner with wife Elizabeth Stewart Warner came to Oregon with the "Lost Wagon Train" and settled on the Middle Fork of the Willamette River, near Fall Creek. They were parents of Frank Warner. The couple took a young Indian boy into their home and raised him as one of their children. His name was Charlie Tufti.

George Warner

George Warner, born in 1860, was the son of Thomas Warner and Agness Stewart Warner who came to Oregon with the "Lost Wagon Train" of 1853. The family lived in the Fall Creek area. George and his wife Vina had a daughter Tracy who was born at Fall Creek in 1888.

Thomas Warner

Thomas Warner came to Oregon as a young man with the "Lost Wagon Train." After settling in Oregon near Fall Creek, he married Agness Stewart who came west with the same wagon train. She was the first teacher in Springfield, Oregon. Three Warner brothers married three Stewart sisters. Thomas Warner married Agness Stewart, Fred Warner married Elizabeth Stewart and John Warner married Mary Stewart. All six of these people came west with the same wagon train.

Clifford E. White

Clifford White married Helen Streit, born December 14, 1923. Helen is the daughter of Ella and Louie Streit. She grew up in Westfir, graduated from Oakridge High School in 1939 and worked one day a week in the Westfir Library. Helen and Clifford have three children — Kenneth, Carla and Barbara. Helen left the Westfir-Oakridge area when she was 20 years old and lives in Everett, Washington.

George R. Willey

George R. Willey, born July 17, 1902, married Mary V. Bowyer on June 13, 1923. Mary was born January 9, 1907. They had one son, Melvin. The Willey family moved to Oakridge in 1941. George worked as a logger for Pope & Talbot from 1946 to 1967 when he retired. George and Mary helped organize the Fir-Oak Minerology Club and were long-time members of the Upper Willamette Pioneer Association. George died January 22, 1984.

Their son Melvin Willey married Thelma Barnes. Thelma and Melvin have two children, Carol Willey Lenocker and James Willey. James married Barbara Brewer.

Mason Williams

Mason Williams went to junior high school (1951–52) and high school (1953–54) in Oakridge. Mason is a noted writer, composer, musician and performer. As a recording artist, Mason won two Grammy Awards in 1968 for his unique composition for guitar, "Classical Gas." Also in 1968, he won an Emmy Award as a television comedy writer for his work on *The Smothers Brothers Comedy Hour*. He has also written and produced books of prose and poetry.

As a performer, Mason has run the gamut from coffee houses to concerts with orchestra including such major symphony orchestras as Denver, Kansas City, New Orleans, Louisville and Edmonton.

In 1969, Mason came home from Hollywood to play a special concert for the annual Tree Planting Festival. Asked to be the Grand Marshal in the parade, Mason opted to appoint "The Honorable Doug Fir" to act on his behalf, thereby making a Douglas Fir the Grand Marshal for that year. In 1984, Mason served as musical director for the historical play "Oakridge Yesterday."

Locally he is known and appreciated for his "Of Time & Rivers Flowing" concerts designed to promote the protection of our rivers.

Mason likes to fly-fish the rivers and streams of the Upper Willamette country whenever his busy schedule allows.

Mason D. Williams was born in 1938 in Abilene, Texas. He first came to the Oakridge-Westfir area on a fishing trip to the North Fork with his parents in 1947. Three years later, the family moved from Oregon City to Oakridge. His stepfather

(Lloyd W. Stevens) drove a logging truck for Oakridge Trucking and his mother (Kathlyn Louise Stevens) was a housewife.

Mason Williams

In 1950, Mason's sister Christy T.A. Stevens was born. Christy attended school in Oakridge, grades 1 through 12, and also took classes at Lane Community College. In 1975, Christy married Michael Kreiling of Oakridge. They live on High Prairie and have two children, Job and Emily. Christy, in addition to being wife and mother, is the vet's assistant and enjoys hunting and fishing with husband Michael, who works for the U.S. Forest Service.

Daniel R. Winfrey

Daniel R. Winfrey was born in 1893 at Hazeldell, Oregon. His mother and father were W.E. and Carrie Winfrey who were living at Hazeldell when the 1900 census was taken. The family was an early day pioneer family on the Upper Willamette.

James E. Wiser

James E. (Jim) Wiser, born February 27, 1908, in Alton, Missouri, married Elizabeth Hendershott on October 31, 1931. Elizabeth was born March 15, 1907, in Yale, Michigan.

Elizabeth worked at Eugene Hospital as an X-ray technician for seven years before moving to Oakridge. Jim went to work for Western Lumber Company at Westfir in 1927 and worked there under the ownerships of Blythe, Westfir Lumber Company and, from 1945 on, Edward Hines Lumber Company. He worked as a utility man on many jobs and for many years as button man or head rig off bearer.

Jim and Elizabeth had two children, James Wiser and Janice Wiser Henning.

Arch Wood

Arch Wood was born September 22, 1875, at Independence, Iowa. In 1899 he married Anna Durkee who was born March 20, 1879, at Independence, Iowa. They were the parents of Maurice Wood who was born in 1905 in Iowa. The family came to Oakridge in 1911. Arch was a carpenter. He built, owned and operated the first hotel in Oakridge from 1912 to 1960. Oakridge school was held in the Wood's Hotel kitchen in 1911. The old Wood's Hotel was the favorite eating place of the train crews that stopped in Oakridge.

Anna died in 1968. Arch died in 1961.

Maurice Wood

Maurice Wood, born 1905 at Independence, Iowa, came to the Oakridge area in 1911. He had a house built on the same lot where his father's hotel stood for 50 years.

William Henry Wolf

William Henry Wolf was born in 1860 in Iowa. He came to the Upper Willamette in 1908. His wife was Susan Burchard who was born 1870 in Tennessee. They lived on the Upper Willamette from 1908 until 1935. William was a powder man for the Forest Service. Their children were Bertha (Hadley), Rose (Condon), Arthur, Pearl, Altadena (married Harry Dale in 1930, he died, in 1932, married Claude Hebert in 1937) and sixth child Boy A. Wolf.

Oral Allen Woodruff

Oral A. Woodruff, born October 18, 1887, in Cody, Nebraska, and Cherriet Karnes, born December 30, 1891, were married at Slate Creek, Idaho, in 1910. They moved to Oakridge in 1923.

Oral had a large team of horses which he used to get out poles from Huckleberry Creek on High Prairie. He also worked for the Forest Service building roads. Later he was a faller and bucker for Westfir Lumber Company and Pope & Talbot.

When they came to Oakridge, the post office was in the Smith store near Salmon Creek Bridge.

Cherriet and Oral had four children who all went to school in Oakridge. The children were:

Heral (Woody) A. Woodruff, born 1911, married Leota Zander. They had a son Michael Allen Woodruff.

Elizabeth (Beth), born May 12, 1917, married Walter Sharp and they had three children, James, Cherriet and Jacqueline (Armstrong). James Sharp had four children, Bill, Mary Beth, Darren and Jennifer. Jacqueline had three children, Angela, Terri and Christopher.

Donna, born November 7, 1919, married Noell Nelson and had two children, Nadine (Strayer) and Louise (Brown).

Vaughn (Ike), born May 28, 1930, married Lois Goforth and they had three children, Janis (Hancock), Dane and Rick Woodruff.

Cherriet was a member of Elm Rebekah Lodge and Upper Willamette Pioneer Association. Oral died in 1966 and Cherriet died in 1980. Both were buried at Forestvale Memorial Park.

Harry S. Worth

Harry Worth, born August 21, 1916, in Amarillo, Texas, and Mary Ellen Triplett were married in 1936. Mary Ellen and Harry had one son, Franklin S. Worth. Franklin is a professional engineer, Chief, Facility Siting Section of Bonneville Power Administration. Franklin's wife Susan McCorkell-Worth, R.D., is a health care specialist in the food service field.

Harry came to Oakridge in 1951. He opened and operated Oakridge Automotive Supply. He had a building built on Highway 58 for the business which he had for 27 years. He sold in 1978.

Harry was active in civic affairs from the time he moved to the area. He was a past President of the Chamber of Commerce, past President of Upper Willamette Pioneer Association, past President of Lane County Chamber of Commerce, served 15 years on Lane County Parks advisory committee and served 15 years on the Oakridge City Council. He was Oakridge Citizen of the Year in 1962. He is a life member of the Masonic Lodge and a member of the United Methodist Church. He has served the church in many capacities over the years.

In 1972, Harry and Mary Ellen were divorced and in 1975 Harry and Veryl Marie Jensen were married.

Veryl was born in 1921 to Rose and Clarence Fowler of Kelso, Washington. She had three children, Ruby M. (Heckes), Shirley J. (Morgan-Brady) and Lewis Scott Wooley, a systems analyst.

Veryl worked as an office manager and accountant. After moving to Oakridge in 1967, she wrote *Early Days on the Upper Willamette,* printed by Myrtle Creek Mail and proceeds going to the Upper Willamette Pioneer Association for the Oakridge Museum. The book was published in 1970 and 3,750 copies were sold.

Veryl was also author of *Willow Pattern China, A Collectors Guide,* first and second edition and co-author of the third edition. She was editor of *Willow News* from 1972 to 1984. Veryl was a Citizen of the Year in 1972, served as Chamber of Commerce secretary and is a member of the United Methodist Church, Arts & Crafts Guild of Oregon, the LaDu-Fowler Family Association and Daughters of the American Revolution, Lewis and Clark Chapter.

Jacob Charles Wright

Jacob Charles Wright was born in 1880 in Emporia, Kansas, and came to Oakridge in 1924. He was the owner of a motel, service station and grocery store located where Dink's Market is now. He also operated a barber shop in Oakridge for six years and owned the shop for 20 years.

He married Minnie B. Madaris in 1907. She was born in 1883 at Chesterfield, Illinois. She was an Oakridge correspondent for the *Eugene Register-Guard* for five years and was the first elected city treasurer. Minnie rode the first train over the mountain to Klamath Falls. Jacob and Minnie were the parents of Charles Walter Wright, who married Beulah Pelzel, and Florence Elisabeth Wright.

Bibliography

1. Claeyssens, Paul G. *Kovdahl 'Dam': Private Enterprise, Forest Policy and Early 20th Century Water Resource Development in Oregon's West-Central Cascades;* Willamette National Forest, Eugene, Oregon, 1988

2. Overland, Wally, *The Maverick Indian: Charlie Tufti;* undated manuscript, 1965–66?

3. Land Deed Document of 1862 #1687 to Charlie Tufti 1884

4. Personal Interview: Harry Clark, Oakridge, Oregon, August 1989

5. Personal Interview: L.L. Stewart, Eugene, Oregon, August 1989

6. Personal Interview: C.B. McFarland, Oakridge, Oregon, September 1967

7. Andrews, Ralph W., *Glory Days of Logging, First Edition,* Superior Publishing Co., Seattle, Washington

8. Gray, Edward, *An Illustrated History of North Klamath County Oregon,* ISBN 0 89288 148 8, Maverick Publications, Bend, Oregon

9. LaLande, Jeff, *A Wilderness Journey with John B. Waldo, Oregon's First "Preservationist,"* Oregon Historical Quarterly, Summer 1989

10. Coleman, E.T. Jr., and H.M. Gibbs, *Time, Tide & Timber, Over a Century of Pope & Talbot,* revised edition 1978, Chapter 15, The Post War Era

11. Ski West, PNSA Publication, April 13, 1951, Page 3, *Skiing Family Style*

12. Fortune, Frances Bates, *The LaDuke Family,* 1988, Lawrence Wesley Owens, 1988

Index

Abernathy, Governor 73
Abrams, Isabelle Warner 125
Addington, L.L. 47
Adkison, Florence 80
Agee, Raymond M. 89
Aiken, Dr. 66
Alexander, Faye 8, 64
Allard, Elsie G. 125
Allard, Franci 83
Allard, Winston 125
Allen, Alta (Racy) 85
Allen, Ann (Swaryck) 85
Allen, Clarence 85
Allen, Ezra Monroe (Ed) 49, 85
Allen, Mildred M. 108
Allen, Mr. 26
Allen, Naomi (Thurman) 85
Allen, Robert 85
Allen, Ulas 85
Allen, W. W. 48
Allen, William 45
Anderson, Archie 67
Anderson, Bud 63
Anderson, Buford 112
Anderson, Dr. David 66
Anderson, Dennis 112
Anderson, Paula 112
Anderson, Rev. 55
Anderson, Sharyle 87
Andrews, Ralph W. 130
Angelos, Dr. 66
Anthony, James 31, 43
Anthony, Jimmy 52
Anthony, Julie 83
Armstrong, Andrea 64
Armstrong, Angela 128
Armstrong, Christopher 128
Armstrong, Jacqueline 128
Armstrong, Nancy 64
Armstrong, Terri 128
Ash, J. D. 58
Ashcraft, Perry A. 19
Ashley, Ida 45
Ashley, James 26
Ashley, Sam 45
Ayres, Echo 118
Ayres, John 118
Ayres, Michelle 118
Ayres, Monica 118
Bacon, Dorothy 104
Bailey, Clara 81
Bailey, Don 111
Bailey, Grace 108
Bailey, Marvin 81
Bain, Cleone 117
Baird, Donna 91
Balander, Judy 48
Ballard, Ivan P. 58
Barber, Chris 64
Barbier, Jeff 85
Barbier, Robin Kay (McFarland) ... 85
Barbare, Veda 51
Barnes, Bruce 85
Barnes, George 42–43
Barnes, Thelma 126

Barstad, Kristin 64
Barstad, Robert L. 25
Barton, Ron 54
Barton, Ruby 54
Barton, Russell 54
Bascom, John 57
Bates 88
Batson, Sheryl 112
Baxter, Fred 97
Baxter, Stella Blakely 52
Baylis, Margaret 107
Bayly, Arthur 63
Beach, Charles L. 25, 48
Beach, Esther 69
Beamer, Roy 8–9
Beard, Marion Douglas 85
Beard, Marion Hugh 85
Beard, Michael Edward 85
Beard, Patricia A. (West) 83, 85
Beasley, Richard 8
Beckman, Don 81
Bedell, "Dude" 36
Bedell, Ted 36
Behr, Charles Alan 85
Behr, Cho Kyong Cha 85
Behr, Diana Emilia 85
Behr, Helga (Enkeboll) 79, 85
Behr, John Edward 85
Behr, Julie Ann 85
Behr, Richard "Dick" .. 38, 63, 71, 85
Bell, Miss Erma 74
Belshaw 15
Belyea, A.M. 42
Bennett, R. S. 21
Bensen, Ben J. 98
Bensen, Ruth 98
Benson, Dr. Joseph 65
Bergeson, Paula 98
Bernard, Bee 31
Bernhart, Howard 114
Bernhart, Olive (Mrs. Howard) ... 114
Bianchini, Dr. Louis 65
Bigger, Linda 83
Biles, Amy 97
Biles, David 97
Bingham, Cy L. 24
Bjorling, Dorothy 86
Bjorling, Ethel 86
Bjorling, Victor 86
Black, Addison 47, 108
Black, Amos 60
Black, Emma Belle Pengra 86
Black, Mr. 125
Black, Steven L. 86
Blair, Mildred Croner .. 48, 93, 98
Blakely, Bonnie (Heimburger) 86
Blakely, Carl 42
Blakely, Elizabeth (Lizzie) 86
Blakely, Ella 86
Blakely, Emmett 86
Blakely, Eula 86
Blakely, Flora 86
Blakely, Frank 86
Blakely, Isabelle 86
Blakely, Jane 86

Blakely, Joe 86
Blakely, John 86
Blakely, Joseph 86
Blakely, Lawrence 86
Blakely, Leona (Wilcox) 86
Blakely, Mattie (Hebert) 86
Blakely, Mary 52, 86
Blakely, Mrs. 47
Blakely, Stella 86
Blakely, Thomas 86
Blakely, Walter 34, 51, 86
Blakely, William 86
Blanton, Leo 51
Blodgett, L. D. 55
Bloom, Ann Marie 119
Blunk, Mary Jane (Kate) 106
Blythe, Witter and Company .. 29–30
Boeckman, Mrs. Wayne 108
Bolin, Amy 103
Bolin, Patti 66
Bolton, Roy 97
Bolton, Ruby 97
Bones, Ruth 112
Boots, H. Harlan 121
Boots, Wilma 121
Bottoms, Shirley 92
Bouhey, Artie Zoe (McGill) 87
Bouhey, Georges F. 42–43, 66, 87
Bouhey, Georges Joel 87
Bouhey, Georges Maurice 87
Bouhey, Joy D. (Lee) 87
Bouhey, Kristen 87
Bouhey, Sharyle (Anderson) 87
Bowerman, Bill 65
Bowerman, Mae 91
Bowles, Boyde 58
Bowyer, Mary V. 126
Boyce, Ken 64
Bradley, Art 66
Bradley, Marjorie 104
Bradley, Roy L. 104
Brady, Shirley J. Morgan 129
Brainard, James 118
Brainard, Phyllis 118–119
Breckel, Suzie 83
Brewer, Barbara 126
Brewer, Carolyn L. 87
Brewer, Christopher 87
Brewer, Genevieve (Sims) 87, 119
Brewer, Karen Marie 87
Brewer, Robert E., Jr. 87
Brewer, Robert E., Sr. 87
Brewer, Rodney A. 87
Brewer, Shayla 87
Brieske, Jane 66
Briggs, Sophronia 101
Bristow, Elijah 19, 47, 73, 76
Bristow, Melvin 19
Broadbent, Susan 53
Brock, Jessie 8–9
Brooks, Art 43
Broome, Steve 64
Brown 66
Brown, Dan 96
Brown, Edith Ryker 118

Brown, Dr. Hughes 66	Chuck Chuck, Jim 3, 108	Clifford, Albert E. "Al" 71, 90
Brown, Louise 128	Churan, Ruth 116	Clifford, Brock 90
Brown, W. O. 22	Ciesiel, Marla 121	Clifford, Gaye (Luna) 90
Bucholtz, Jean 48	Claeyssens, Paul G. 60, 130	Clifford, John E. "Jack" 90
Buckenhams 5	Clark, Allen R. 90	Clifford, Mary "Betty" (Hugill) 71, 90, 104
Buckner, Paula 83	Clark, Andy 111	Clifford, Patricia (Wells) 90
Buettner, Fredrick 56	Clark, Aulene 89	Clifford, Sherene (Crager) 90
Bunnell, Margaret 93	Clark, Baby 90	Clifford, Susan (Fields) 90
Burby, Jim 64	Clark, Barbara (Tatro) 89	Clifford, Tamaris (Rogers) .. 71, 90, 117
Burchard, Susan 128	Clark, Bert 74	Cline 5
Burgan, W. J. 42	Clark, Bessie B. 90	Cline, Curtis 111
Burgen, Gale 83	Clark, Carol 7	Cline, George 64
Burgess, Bud 79	Clark, Catherine 89	Cole, Phil 63
Burke, Robert 43	Clark, Charles E. 88–89	Coleman, E. T., Jr. 130
Burr, Larry 66	Clark, Charles Edward (Ed) 62, 74, 88, 125	Collins, G. D. 8
Burton 112	Clark, Christine 89	Collins, Liz 8
Bushong, Jill 83	Clark, Cindy 88	Condon, Rose 128
Butler, Gay 117	Clark, Clara 51	Conner, Arlie B., Rev. 56
Butler, Scott 97	Clark, Dale 88	Conner, David 56
Cain, Beulah 51	Clark, Dale Randal 88	Conner, Fae 56
Cain, Edith 52, 94	Clark, Dareld J. 90	Conner, Violet 56
Cain, Elsie 52	Clark, Denise 111	Cook, Dean 54
Cain, Ferril Amanda 51, 109	Clark, Dennis 89	Cook, Ellen 54
Cain, Harley 11, 29, 51	Clark, Dewayne 89	Cook, Harry 54
Cain, Harvey 51	Clark, Donald R. 89	Cook, Lawrence 42, 63
Cain, Iva 51	Clark, Dorothy 90	Cook, Lloyd 54
Cain, Ivy 52	Clark, Douglas M. 89	Cook, Sue 54
Cain, John 70	Clark, Earl 76, 89, 115	Cooledge, V. R. 21
Cain, Margaret Lewis 94	Clark, Earl H. 90	Cooney, Benjamin W. 88
Cain, Maude 51	Clark, Ellen Irene 89	Cooney, Irene 87–88
Cain, Methias 94	Clark, Elvina (Neyman) 89	Cooper, Art 64, 90–91
Cain, Roy 36, 51, 52	Clark, Esther 8	Cooper, Doris 90–91
Calleman, Bertie 45	Clark, Ethel Amelia 89	Cornish, Sherryl 89
Cameron, L. A. 47	Clark, Eula Mary 50, 89	Cowart 112
Campbell, Bev 8	Clark, Flora M. (Pugh) 89	Crager, Sherene 90
Campbell, Irene Cooney 87–88	Clark, Gary D. 89	Crahan, Joe 54
Campbell, J. F. 25	Clark, Gloria J. 89	Craig, Bob 54
Campbell, Joseph V. (Van) 88	Clark, Goldie 50	Cramer, Scott 8
Campbell, Leslie Perkins 88	Clark, Harry 38–41, 43–44, 71, 79, 89, 130	Crandall, Ronald 8, 64, 82
Campbell, Mark Thomas 88	Clark, Hobart Aliska 89–90	Craydon, Margaret 95
Campbell, Sharon L. Carlisle 88	Clark, Irvin "Bud" 89	Crist, Al 36, 91
Campbell, Waldo J. 87	Clark, Irvin D. 89	Crist, Dave 91
Carlino, Mary Jane 108	Clark, Irvin McClellan 89	Crist, Donald J. 91
Carlisle, Robert L. 88	Clark, Jerry R. 89	Crist, Donna (Baird) 91
Carlisle, Sharon L. 88	Clark, John Albert 89	Crist, James 91
Carter, A. 36	Clark, Judy (Page) 89	Crist, John 91
Carter, Joe 35	Clark, Katherine (McClintock) 89	Crist, Katherine (McKenzie) 91
Carter, Lucile 48	Clark, Kenneth R. 89	Crist, Katheryn 91
Carter, Margaret 111	Clark, Larry G. 89	Crist, Nancy (Stears) 91
Carter, Thelma 125	Clark, LeRoy 89	Crist, Peggy 91
Cartwright, John 78	Clark, Louise 64, 88, 125	Crist, Tony 91
Cartwright, Margaret 78	Clark, Martha 99	Croner, Barbara 70
Cartwright, Vivian 47, 76	Clark, Martin 86	Croner, Charles 63, 93
Carver, Gail (John) 43	Clark, Martin Aliska 89	Croner, Charlie 38
Carver, Ken, Dr. 7	Clark, Maude Catherine 89	Croner, Lois Mae 71, 93
Cash, Bill 81	Clark, Mildred 89, 92	Croner, Mildred 93
Caskey, Virgil 55	Clark, Milton James 89	Crook, Claire (Thomen) 91
Castleman, Ivy 108	Clark, Olive (Sutherlin) 89	Crook, George 91
Chambers, George 118	Clark, Randie 88	Cross, Alma 56
Chambers, Mildred 118	Clark, Raymond C. 8, 46, 89, 90	Cross, Charles 117
Chan, M.B. 22	Clark, Ruth 89, 115	Cross, Elza 56
Chaney, Ida 95	Clark, Sherryl (Cornish) 89	Cross, Mrs. Elza 56
Chaplin, Marjorie 104	Clark, Stephen 89	Cross, Harold 56, 64
Chenoweth, Edith 88	Clark, Terry R. 89	Cross, Marjorie 117
Chenoweth, Frank 88	Clark, Thomas Volney 89	Cross, Mark 117
Chenoweth, James 88	Clark, Velma Luella (Williams) 89	Cross, Mathew 117
Chenoweth, Thelma 51, 88	Clark, Wayne E. 90	Cross, Michael 56
Christy, W. 73	Clark, William McKinley 89	Cross, Michelle 117

Name	Page
Cross, Mike	117
Crumb, Ivan W.	25
Cruzatte, Peter	73
Culbertson, Alice E.	91
Culbertson, Diane E.	91
Culbertson, Dick	91
Culbertson, Joanne L.	91
Culbertson, Mae Bowerman	91
Culbertson, Mark R.	91
Culbertson, Richard	64
Cunningham, Lisa Pauleen	92
Cunningham, Lyle Phillip	92
Cunningham, Lyle Porter	92
Cunningham, Mildred L. Clark	92
Cummins, William (Bill)	25, 83
Currier, Clarence	58
Dale, Altadina	128
Dale, Harry	128
Dappert, Hans	57
Darby, Del	57
Darling	105
David, Jake	57
Davidson, David	92,
Davidson, Diane Dalton	92
Davidson, Jerald	92
Davidson, John	92
Davidson, Leslie L.	92
Davidson, Myrtle Price	92
Davidson, Roy	92
Davidson, Shirley	92
Davies, Elsie	98
Davies, Jessie	98
Davis, Ann Jeanette	92
Davis, Bert	8, 36, 71, 92
Davis, Iola	69, 92
Davis, John L.	54
Davis, Roberta, R.N.	92
Davis, Thelma	104
Dean, Alvin	92–93, 107
Dean, Elizabeth Wert	92
Dean, Flora	92
Dean, Freda (Dillard)	92
Dean, Gary R.	92
Dean, Howard R.	92
Dean, Loretta Rae	92
Dean, Mary C.	92, 107
Dean, Momikai (Mount)	93, 110
Dean, Orville B.	92
Dean, Penny Lou	92
Dean, Robert A.	92–93, 110
Dean, Terry R.	92
Dean, Vicki Horner	92–93, 107
DeHarpport, Dennis	64
DeLong, Pam	8, 64
DeLong, Phillip	8
DeLong, Sasha	8
Demagalski, Janet	83
Denison, June	97
Dennison, Alice	45
Denny, Julie	117
Denny, Michael	117
Denny, Patti Bergman	117
Dentel, Karen (Woolery)	93
Dentel, Michelle	93
Dentel, Niki	93
Dentel, Phyllis (Fleischman)	8, 93
Dentel, Stephen Dale	93
Dentel, Thomas William	93
Dentel, Vicki (Z'berg)	93
Dentel, William C. (Bill)	93
DeVogele, Alisha R.	93
DeVogele, Beth McFarland	93
DeVogele, Valere M. Marc	93
DeVogele, Valere Marcel, R.P.	93
DeWitt, Dr.	65
Diamond, John	74
Dick, Doug	32, 37
Diess, Iris	93
Diess, Ivan	93
Diess, Karen L.	93
Diess, Lois Mae (Croner)	70, 93
Diess, Neil E., M.D.	65, 93
Diess, Richard C.	93
Diess, Susan C.	93
Dillard, Alfred	54
Dillard, Candace	51
Dillard, Freda	92
Dobbins, Dr.	65
Dompier, Felix	41
Dompier, Flora Warner	125
Dompier, Frank	11–13
Dooley, Diane	112
Dooley, Margaret	64
Doppee, Cherie	111
Dorfler, Fred	63, 66
D'Orsay, Catherine	89
Doty, Ormond H.	25
Downes, Dr. Joseph	65
Drake, Donald	63
Drake, Frank	68
Draper, Andy J.	17, 19, 57, 93
Draper, Brian	94
Draper, Erik	93
Draper, Jerald	93
Draper, Margaret Bunnell	93
Draper, Melvin	93
Draper, Phillip	93
Draper, Sharon Kenyon	93
Draper, Susan (Rasmussan)	93
Drumm, Maxine	48
Dude, Clare	97
Dugger, Joe	36
DuMont, A.	55
DuMont, Bill	71
Dunn, Sarah	48
Dunn, William A.	66
Dunning, Anna (Jeske)	94
Dunning, Charles Marion	94
Dunning, Clara (Prokop)	94
Dunning, D.	47
Dunning, Harold Holt	94
Dunning, Iola M.	92–94
Dunning, Joanna	94, 116
Dunning, Mercy (Holt)	94
Dunning, Mr.	24
Dunning, Ralph M.	94
Dunning, Raymond	49, 55
Dunning, Raymond L.	94
Dunning, Robert "Hop"	34, 94
Dunning, Robert Charles	94
Durand, Shawnna	83
Durbin, Martin S.	25
Durkee, Anna	128
Dutton	88
Dyer, Jim	64
Eaton, Bill	37
Eaton, Dora A. (Glaspey)	94
Eaton, Ed	36
Eaton, Edith	94
Eaton, Edward	94
Eaton, Edward Warren	94
Eaton, Genevieve (Rutherford)	94
Eaton, Thelma (Hamilton)	94
Eaton, Will	94
Eby, Don	56
Edbloom, Phil	80
Eddy, Walt	47
Edie, Effie	54
Edie, Levi	54
Edwards, Elizabeth	122
Edwards, Major R. L.	2
Edwards, Robert	122
Ehinger, Paul Jr.	28
Ehinger, Paul	31
Elam, Marlene	83
Elkington, Grant	58
Elliot, Mrs. C. R.	55
Elliot, Roy	79
Elliott, Rae	111
Ellis, Virginia	56
Elsworth	15
Emerson, Anor	54
England, Dorris	52
Enkeboll, Helga	85
Ensminger, Dale	62
Eskridge, Mamie	118
Evans, Lisa	92
Evans, Michael J.	92
Evans, Nikki Luella	92
Evers, Colleen	118
Ezawa, Fumiko	110
Falkner, L.	47
Farrell, Margaret	95
Farrier, Raquel	83
Faulk, Marshall	55
Faust, Bill "Bull Pine"	36
Fenton, Effa	50
Ferrigno, Paul	56
Ferrin, Bill	28–29
Fields, Joseph	74
Fields, Reuben	74
Fields, Susan	90
Filter, Amy E.	88
Filter, Andrew	88
Filter, Gina	88
Filter, Gregory	88
Filter, Kayla	88
Filter, Lauren	88
Fisher, Dona	85
Fisher, Eleanor (Mrs. Osburn)	114
Fisher, Elena	8
Fleischaker, Herbert	29
Fleischman, Phyllis	93
Fleming, Ilena	82
Flock, Ada M.	95
Flock, Alva Willard	95
Flock, Clara M.	95
Flock, Emma N.	95
Flock, Ida Chaney	95
Flock, Inez	117
Flock, James Louis	94–95, 118
Flock, Jesse E.	95
Flock, Lina	8–9, 94, 118, 125
Flock, Lora Sharp	95

Flock, Louis	Gray, Francis	Hansen, Frederick
8–9	96	98
Flock, Mamie … 47	Gray, Israel J. … 1, 74, 95, 113, 125	Hansen, Janet … 83
Flock, Margaret Craydon … 95	Gray, Margaret (Farrell) … 95	Hansen, Orvel Jr. … 98
Flock, Mary Ellen … 95, 122	Gray, Olive May … 95, 125	Hansen, Orvel Sr. … 98
Flock, Mildred … 94, 118	Gray, Stanley Ira … 95	Hansen, Pamela (Henderson) … 98
Flock, Orlo Alva … 94	Gray, Mrs. T. … 47	Hansen, Ryan Joel … 98
Flock, Roy … 24–25	Gray, Theresa … 95, 125	Hansen, Wendy … 98
Flock, Samuel L. … 95	Gray, Thomas J. … 47	Hanson, Amy … 98
Flock, Sara Edna (Raymond) … 95	Greer, Aaron … 97	Hanson, Heide Sue … 98
Flock, Viola Osborn … 95	Greer, Family … 56	Hanson, Jim … 56
Flock, William … 95	Greer, Georgia … 96	Hanson, Linda … 98
Flock, William P. … 95	Greer, Joyce … 97	Hanson, Violet … 56
Flynn … 66	Greer, June … 97	Hanson, Zachary … 98
Follet, Sharon … 111	Greer, Kristen … 97	Hapner, Vernon … 52
Forbis, Eldon … 63–64	Greer, Linda … 97	Haralson, Bruce … 97
Fortune, Frances Bates … 130	Greer, Mary (Heywood) … 97	Haralson, Elizabeth … 96
Foster, Billy … 52	Greer, Max. A. … 96	Hardin, Claude … 36
Fowler, Clarence … 129	Greer, Onata … 96	Hardin, John … 78
Fowler, Rose … 129	Greer, Randy … 97	Harding, Brothers … 36
Fox, Ida … 111	Greer, Rev. … 55	Harkins, Harvey … 62–63
Frame, Max … 67	Greer, Sandra … 97	Harmon, Paul … 63
Fredricks, Richard L. … 66	Greer, Sheila … 97	Harp, Gloria D. … 112
Fredrickson, Pauline … 123	Greer, Sunny … 97	Harris, Helen M. … 112
Frederickson, Carol … 7	Greer, Tammy … 97	Harris, Leroy … 56
Frederickson, Deanna … 111	Greer, Velma … 97	Harris, Dr. Waldo E. … 65, 104, 123
Frederickson, Oscar … 19	Greyell, Rev. … 55	Harvey, Bessie Louise … 125
Freeland, Gus … 47	Griffith, George … 38	Harvey, Roy … 47, 125
Fuchec, L. … 43	Griffith, Dr. Warren … 66	Haskett, Audrey … 117
Fulton … 88	Grundeman, M. R. … 31	Haskett, Marie … 117
Furnish, James L. … 25, 74	Gullion, Dr. Omar … 80	Haskett, Thomas … 117
Gale, Lauren A. … 95	Hadley, Alene … 8	Hatfield, Billie … 116
Gale, Lauren H. … 95	Hadley, Bertha … 128	Hawes … 66
Galla Logging Co. … 36	Hadley, Edwin … 8, 64	Hayes, Roger … 43
Garcia, Joanne … 98	Haffner, Dr. Wesley … 65	Haynes, Al … 43
Garcia, Tom … 98	Hamilton, Squire … 74	Hays, Fred … 48
Garcia, Troy … 98	Hamilton, Thelma Eaton … 94	Hebert, Alberta Patrick … 99
Gardner, Craig … 56	Hamilton, Wilma … 101	Hebert, Altadena … 128
Gardner, Dale … 64	Hamlin, Dorr … 80	Hebert, Boyd … 99
Gardner, Jill … 56	Hammerschmith, W. N. … 42	Hebert, Mrs. Boyd … 47
Gastawbide, Blanche … 110	Hammock, Jessica … 97	Hebert, Charles … 98
Gerimonte, A. E. … 55, 95	Hammock, Sheila … 97	Hebert, Charles E. … 47, 70, 98–99
Gerimonte, Esther … 95	Hammock, Tony … 97	Hebert, Clarence R. … 28, 98–99
George, James … 47	Hamner, Amy … 51, 97	Hebert, Claude … 99, 128
Gerspach, Lorenz … 62–63	Hamner, Angelina … 97	Hebert, Cleo … 98
Gibbs, H. M. … 130	Hamner, Carl … 51, 97	Hebert, Clifford … 99
Gibson, Swede … 36	Hamner, Clair … 51	Hebert, Curtis … 98
Gilbert … 74	Hamner, Clare (Dude) … 97	Hebert, Daisy Bell … 97
Gilbert, Bill … 57	Hamner, Daisy Bell Hebert … 97	Hebert, Daisy Lee Gray … 95, 99
Gilbert, Nanette … 111	Hamner, Dale … 51, 97	Hebert, Darrell … 99
Gillespie, Debbie … 8	Hamner, Evelyn … 97	Hebert, Delbert … 99
Gillespie, Jim … 64	Hamner, Mrs. G. W. … 47	Hebert, Della Holesclaw … 99
Gillespie, Kathie … 83	Hamner, Isaac … 47, 76, 97	Hebert, Dorothy June … 99
Gilliam, Patsy … 64, 122	Hamner, Joyce … 97	Hebert, Edward … 98
Goddard, Aline … 8	Hamner, Kenneth … 97	Hebert, Elsie … 98
Goddard, Joe … 8	Hamner, Lucille Praces … 97	Hebert, Ernest … 98–99
Goddard, Nancy … 8	Hamner, Ruby … 51, 97	Hebert, Ernie … 12, 36
Goforth, Lois … 128	Hamner, Walter G. … 97	Hebert, Ethel (Singletary) … 98–99
Gold, Mr. … 74	Hampton, Don … 8	Hebert, Family … 41, 45
Gonet, Ryan J. … 110	Hancock, Janis … 128	Hebert, Faye … 99
Goodson, L. J. … 47	Handsaker, Samuel … 47	Hebert, Frieda … 98
Gosnell, Florence … 96	Hankins, Irene … 98	Hebert, George E. … 45, 95, 98–99
Gosnell, Florence (Henry) … 96	Hankins, Paul … 98	Hebert, Gladys … 98
Gosnell, Max … 64, 96	Hankins, Paula (Bergeson) … 98	Hebert, Glen … 98
Gosnell, Sandra (Pyles) … 96	Hankins, Richard … 98	Hebert, Harry … 99
Graham, Bertha … 64	Hannell, Otto B. … 25	Hebert, Hazel … 51, 98
Gray, Daisy Lee … 95, 99	Hansen, Burt … 98	Hebert, James Clark … 99
Gray, Edward … 130	Hansen, Charlie … 67	Hebert, Jennie … 70, 98
Gray, Elizabeth (Haralson) … 96	Hansen, Evelyn (Walters) … 48, 98	Hebert, Joanne (Garcia) … 98

Hebert, LaVelle	98	
Hebert, Leanne	98	
Hebert, LeRoy	99	
Hebert, Lewis	99	
Hebert, Libby	83	
Hebert, Margery	99	
Hebert, Martha Clark	99	
Hebert, Mattie	86	
Hebert, Myrle	98	
Hebert, Nellie Holt	51, 99	
Hebert, Nelly	47	
Hebert, Peter	45, 47, 99	
Hebert, Rigmore (Johnson)	64, 98–99	
Hebert, Ruth	98	
Hebert, Stacy	98	
Hebert, V. F.	49	
Hebert, Vera Margaret	99	
Hebert, Vertie (Bert)	99	
Hebert, Virgil	99	
Hebert, William	45, 99	
Heckes, Ruby M.	129	
Heidrich, Marion	42	
Heimburger, Bonnie Blakely	86	
Hein, Emilie	104	
Heinz, Courtney J.	99	
Heinz, Erin Murphy	99	
Heinz, Jean (McFarland), R.D.	99	
Heinz, Stanley Edward	99	
Heinz, Stephanie A.	99	
Helikson, Beth Ann	100	
Helikson, Dale E., J.D.	7, 63, 64, 66, 99, 100	
Helikson, Helen Jean	64, 100	
Helikson, Hubert Taylor	100	
Helikson, Martha (Pauly)	100	
Helikson, Mary Alice	100	
Helikson, Mary Kathryn	7, 64, 99–100	
Helikson, Susan Kay	100	
Hemm, Bruce	64	
Hendershott, Elizabeth	127	
Henderson, LaVelle	98	
Henderson, Pamela	98	
Hendrickson, Dan	71	
Hendrickson, Larry	71	
Henning, Janice Wiser	127	
Henry, Florence	96	
Henry, Lisa	111	
Henry, Shane	8, 111	
Hensen, Fred	41	
Hensen, Molly	41	
Hensley, Pamela Sue	102	
Herbst, Tom	67	
Herndon, Etta (Mrs. Virgil)	114	
Hess	56	
Heywood, Mary	97	
Hickman, Al	57	
Hiett, Mr.	51	
Higgins, Dr. Herbert	95	
High, Bud	64	
Hill, Frances	18	
Hill, Jim	64, 105	
Hill, John	25, 45, 47, 75, 100–101	
Hill, John H.	75	
Hill, Penny	83	
Hill, Phoebe Warfield	75, 100–101	
Hill, Ruth	89	
Hill, William James (Billy)	100–101	
Hill, Wm.	47	
Hills, Carol	101	
Hills, Charlie	67, 101	
Hills, Cornelius J.	6, 75, 101	
Hills, Debbie	111	
Hills, Elijah	101	
Hills, Flora Neet	8–10, 24, 101, 124	
Hills, Fred	101	
Hills, Grace (Walker)	47, 101, 124	
Hills, Hallie (Huntington)	8–9, 51, 101	
Hills, Heide	101	
Hills, Henrietta (Jacoby)	101	
Hills, Jasper B.	8–10, 24, 35–37, 101, 124	
Hills, Jessie (Humphrey)	101	
Hills, Jessie (Stewart)	101	
Hills, Joel	101	
Hills, John	101	
Hills, Larry	101	
Hills, Lawrence	8–9, 24, 36, 49, 63–64, 88, 101	
Hills, Mary (Smith)	101	
Hills, Molly	101	
Hills, Roy	101	
Hills, Sheridan	101	
Hills, Sophronia (Briggs)	75, 101	
Hills, Vera	50	
Hills, Wilma (Hamilton)	101	
Hines, Charlie	38	
Hines, Edward Lbr. Co.	28	
Hise, Sandra Louise	104	
Hodgdon, Jeanette (Mrs. Paul)	105	
Hoffman, Bruce	28	
Holeman, Dorothy (Johnson)	8, 19	
Holeman, Earl D.	102	
Holeman, Pamela Sue (Hensley)	102	
Holesclaw, Della	99	
Holland, Charles, Dr.	65	
Holland, Crate	52	
Holland, Ivy	52	
Holland, Lawrence	47	
Holland, Nelly	52	
Holly, Mary Ellen	8	
Holly, Teri	64	
Holmes, Gov. Robert	87	
Holst, Amy (Bolin)	103	
Holst, Anna "Effie"	102–103	
Holst, Aubrey	103	
Holst, Carson	102–103	
Holst, Dr.	65	
Holst, Judy Wegge	102	
Holst, Leland	102–103	
Holst, Maurice "Maurie" R.	95, 102	
Holt, Alice	47, 104	
Holt, Barbara (Schmidt)	103	
Holt, Bertha	104	
Holt, Edith	88, 104	
Holt, Emilie Hein	104	
Holt, Florence	49, 104, 120	
Holt, Florence (Miller)	103	
Holt, Gertrude	104	
Holt, Harold	104	
Holt, Helen	104	
Holt, Henry	46, 103	
Holt, Jennie	98, 104	
Holt, John	104	
Holt, John C.	104	
Holt, Lucille	104	
Holt, Mary Vincent	104	
Holt, Mercy (Mertie)	94, 104	
Holt, Nellie	49, 51, 99, 104	
Holt, Nelly	47	
Holt, R. M.	47	
Holt, Randolph	55, 104	
Holt, Sharon (Kutch)	103	
Holt, Walt	36	
Holt, William	104	
Hooker	98	
Hopkins, Rose	64	
Horner, Viola "Vickie"	92	
Horton, Henry	95	
Hovey, Albert	47	
Howard, Lloyd	55, 58, 87	
Hubbard, David	56	
Huff, Dr. Laverne	64, 66	
Hughey, Anna Marie (Spenser)	104	
Hughey, Donald Spenser	104	
Hughey, Judson E.	104	
Hughey, Marjorie (Chaplin)	104	
Hughey, Marsha Anne	104	
Hughey, Sandra Louise (Hise)	104	
Hugill, Al	104	
Hugill, Betty (Clifford)	90, 104	
Hugill, Dorothy (Bacon)	104	
Hugill, Essie Parker	104	
Hugill, James	104	
Hugill, John	104	
Humason, Clara A.	84	
Humphrey, Jeanette (Mrs. Paul) Hodgon	105	
Humphrey, Jessie	101	
Humphrey, Judith (Mrs. Kenneth) Starkbien	105	
Humphrey, Percy Nobel	104–105	
Humphrey, Stanley	105	
Humphrey, Rev. Stanley R.	55, 105	
Humphrey, Stanley Robert	105	
Humphrey, Thelma	66, 105	
Humphrey, Thelma Davis	104	
Hunsaker, Dale, Dr.	65, 104	
Hunsaker, Dan	6	
Hunsaker, Thomas	77	
Huntington, Ed	81	
Huntington, Hallie Hills	9, 101	
Husser, Norman	31, 64	
Hutchins, Frank	51	
Hyland, A. D.	2, 25	
Hyland, Amos	47, 74	
Hyland, Dora	49	
Hyland, Grant	2, 25	
Hyland, Ruth	52, 108–109	
Hyland, Wilbur	36, 47	
Inmon, Jeanne	122	
Inmon, Jeffrey	122	
Irwin, Clara	51	
Iverson, Don	8	
Jackson, Diana	64	
Jackson, Lloyd	58	
Jacoby, Dr.	65	
Jacoby, G. E.	37	
Jacoby, Henrietta	101	
Jacoby, Lester	37	
James, Viola	111	
James, Will	28	
Jellum, Norman	48	
Jenkins	88	
Jenkins, Janet M.	86	
Jenkins, Joby Ryan	86	
Jenkins, John Gregory	105	

Jenkins, Josephine (Stiffy) 105
Jenkins, Sandra Marie 86
Jenkins, Sondra (Whitaker) 105
Jenkins, Tracy Lynn 105
Jenkins, William Gregory (Greg) ... 105
Jenkins, William H................ 105
Jensen, Buck 64
Jensen, Veryl Marie 64, 129
Jerginson, Norman 96
Jeske, Anna 94
Johnson, Betty 122
Johnson, Dr. Carol 64, 66
Johnson, Dinah 97
Johnson, Dorothy 101
Johnson, E. 47
Johnson, Kenneth 52
Johnson, Laura 97
Johnson, Laurie 111
Johnson, Linda 97
Johnson, Murray 97
Johnson, Nancy Ann 121
Johnson, Rigmore 98–99
Johnson, Scott 111
Jones, Bret 118
Jones, Claude R. ....
.... 24–25, 27, 46, 55, 58, 63–64
Jones, Ella M. 116
Jones, J. W. (Bill) 101
Jones, Jim 8, 64
Jones, Karen 118
Jones, Kyle 118
Jones, Marsha 83
Jones, Ruth 8, 64
Jones, Sarah 48
Jones, Rev. Ted 64
Jowers, Dean E. 105, 123
Jowers, Dean Tracy 105
Jowers, Shirley Tracy 105, 123
Julian, Gordon 105
Julian, Janet Marie 105
Julian, Nancy Louise 105
Julian, Phyllis L. McMahon ....
.... 11, 29, 51, 52, 105
Karnes, Cherriet 128
Kearns, Cleo 111
Keefer, Jane 64
Keffer, Dennis 68
Keller, Brian 97
Keller, Dan 112
Keller, Maureen 112
Keller, Scott 112
Keller, Sheila 97
Keller, Ted 112
Kellom, Grace 107
Kelly, George 28–29
Kelly, John 28
Kelsay, Wm. L. 47
Kelsey, Bessie 51
Kelsey, Clayton 51–52
Kelsey, Letha 51–52
Kelsey, Vina 51
Kenyon, Sharon 93
Kincaid, Frank 38
Kingrey, Janet 111
Kissinger 88
Kissinger, Walt 58
Kitson, Dave 75, 80–81, 124
Kitson, David 106

Klein, Eva Mae (Winkelman) 106
Klein, Frank Howard 106
Kloster, Cherri 117
Klosterman, Karen 83
Klosterman, Peter 63
Klosterman, Werner 69
Klovdahl, Simon 60, 75
Knapp, Opal Sears............... 106
Knapp, Roy L. 106
Knapp, Roy P. 106
Knapp, Roy 31
Knight, Joyce 8
Knoop, Margaret Lena 107
Knott, Dorothy 86
Knott, Janet M. (Jenkins) 86
Knott, Karen A. (O'Hearn) 86
Knott, W. R. 86
Koch, L. G. 47
Kolb, W. David 25
Korn, George 79–80
Korstad, Mr. 68
Koskey, Abel 122
Koskey, Audrey 122
Kotch, Louie 12, 75
Kreiling, Christy 127
Kreiling, Emily 127
Kreiling, Job 127
Kreiling, Michael 127
Krueger, Tracy 8
Kutch, Sharon 63, 103
LaBansky 88
LaDuke A. 106
LaDuke, Andrew (Punch) 106
LaDuke, Archie E. 106
LaDuke, Bud 106
LaDuke, C. 106
LaDuke, Chilton L. 106
LaDuke, Don 106
LaDuke, Emery Seymore 106
LaDuke, Emory 106
LaDuke, Leslie 106
LaDuke, Mary Jane (Kate) Blunk .. 106
LaDuke, Michael 106
LaDuke, O. 106
LaDuke, Otto (Spot) 106
LaDuke, Pat 106
LaDuke, Sarah Victoria 106
Lagenor, Doug 64
Lake, Jeffery 66
LaLande, Jeff 130
LaMar, Gertrude Shedd 106
LaMar, William K. 106
Lane, Florence 54
Lansberry, Eileen 52
Large, Mapril 111
Larison, George 35, 75, 106–107
Larison, George W. 106
Larison, Mrs. George W. 86
Larison, Stella Pengra 106
Larwood, Jack 28
Lavoy, Gene 98
Lavoy, Gladys 70, 98
Lawson, Anna 111
Lawton, Rev. 55
Leaming, Cortnee Doreen 107
Leaming, Margaret Baylis 107
Leaming, Robert 107
Leaming, Robert William (Will) ... 107

Leaming, Terry Martin 107
Leaming, Virgil 107
Leavitt, Teddy 54
Lee, Brenda Joy 83, 87
Lee, Frieda 98
Lee, Herbert (Bud) 98
Lee, Ira Val 87
Lee, Joy D. Bouhey 64, 87
Lee, Martin Val 87
Lee, Maurice (Mike) 98
Lee, Myrle 98
Lee, Shawna 83
Lee, Val 105
Leipzig, Father 55
Leith, Hazel 51
Lemons, Howard 31
Lennox, Brandon 121
Lennox, Lindsey 121
Lennox, Susan 121
Lenocker, Carol Willey 126
Lewis, Ada M. 95
Lewis and Clark 73–74
Lewis, Marion 95
Linahan, Father 56
Lincoln, Pres. Abraham 14, 123
Lindke, Evelyn 121
Lindsay, Anna 109
Lindsay, Jeanne 115
Lister, Darlene Faye 122
Lobben, Austin D. 119
Lobben, Cathy L. 119
Long, Bud 36, 69
Long, Jeffery 121
Long, Karen Lynn Svendsen 121
Long, Kyle Jeffery Svendsen ... 121
Long, Neil 52
Long, Margaret McAtee 119
Loudermilk, Verna May 122
Love 5
Lovelady, Ruth 121
Lowell, E. D. 75
Lowen, Earl 54
Lowman, Chuck 28
Lueddemann, Mr. 38
Luna, Gaye 90
Lund, Ruby 62
Lundberg, Brad 111
Lundbom, Amanda 97
Lundbom, Devin 97
Lundbom, Jonathan 97
Lundbom, Joyce 97
Lundbom, Mark 97
Lundbom, Melissa 97
Lunyou, Nadine Evelyn 122
Lyda, Grace Kellom 107
Lyda, Heidi 107
Lyda, Mary Dean 107
Lyda, Paul 107
Lyda, Talana 107
Lyda, Terry 107
Lynch, Anna Marie 107
Lynch, Betty (Oleson) 107
Lynch, Dan 107
Lynch, Dee 107
Lynes, D. 13
Lysne, Michael D. 25
McAtee, Hazel M. Tiller ... 108, 122
McAtee, LeRoy G. 108

McAtee, Margaret 119	McKinney, Melvin 37	Morris, Eva 52
McAtee, Margaret Lena Knoop 107, 108	McKinnis, Charlotte 116	Morris, George A............... 110
McAtee, Mary Jane (Carlino) 108	McMahon, Bobbie Sorenson 65, 109, 119	Morris, George Jackson 23
McAtee, Mildred M. (Allen) 108	McMahon, Brittney Ferral 110	Morris, Joseph Henry 23
McAtee, Minnie E. (Robertson) 108	McMahon, Donald H............. 109	Morris, Joe................... 110
McAtee, Norris N................ 108	McMahon, Edna M. (Strakbein) 109	Morris, John R................. 110
McAtee, Oscar............... 48, 62	McMahon, Evelyn M. 109, 123	Morris, Kevin 110
McAtee, Oscar Benedict 107	McMahon, Ferril Amanda Cain 109	Morris, Pam 110
McAlister, Mrs.................. 81	McMahon, George 47	Morris, Rollo J................. 110
McArthur, Lewis A............... 94	McMahon, Jacob 110	Morris, Sam 52
McBee, Alice 51	McMahon, Kyle 110	Morse, B. Eric 25
McClane, Anna 47	McMahon, Leo 13, 74	Morse, Wayne 105
McClane, Anna May 108	McMahon, Linda Kay 109	Mount, Clyde Parker 93, 110
McClane, Almonza 3, 74, 108	McMahon, Lori Tomlin 64, 110	Mount, Fumiko (Ezawa) 93, 110
McClane, Charles................ 73	McMahon, Phyllis (Julian) . 52, 105, 109	Mount, Momikai Ezawa 92, 110
McClane, Charles E.............. 108	McMahon, Shelby 110	Mount, Robert Ezawa 110
McClane, Geneva 108	McMahon, Susan K 110	Murray, Kellie 121
McClane, Grace Bailey 108	McMahon, William A., Jr......... 109	Murry, Keith................... 57
McClane, Harriet Wilcox 108	McMahon, William D......... 109-110	Myklebust, John 54
McClane, Ivy Castleman 108	McMasters, Edna Tiner 52	Nagtegaal, G. P................. 22
McClane, John 8, 9, 108	McMasters, Mick 49	Naro, Cherie A. Doppee......... 111
McClane, John Harold 108	McPherson, Frank 43	Naro, Chester C................ 111
McClane, Mark 108	McPherson, Mikal 83	Naro, Dacia 111
McClane, Mary 108	Madarís, Minnie B.............. 129	Naro, Dale A.................. 111
McClane, Thomas 108	Maddox, Art 8	Naro, Danae 111
McClintock, Katherine 89	Marconi, John 82	Naro, Dane 111
McCorkell, Susan................ 129	Mardini, Chas.................. 47	Naro, Darrell L................. 111
McCready, Bill 79	Martin, Terry 107	Naro, David C................. 111
McCredie, W. W............. 75-79	Martinson, Bill 64	Naro, David N................. 111
McCully, Beverly 64	Marusich, Carol 66	Naro, Debbie Perkins 111
McCurdy, Ralph E. 25	Matheny, Charles 108	Naro, Derek 111
McDougal, Brothers 36	Mathews, Earnie 49	Naro, Dezerae J................ 111
McDowell, B.................... 47	Mays, Joe 54	Naro, Judy Pflughaupt 111
McDowell, Elizabeth Warner 125	Mays, Wilma 121	Naro, Mapril Large 111
McFarland, Al 74	Mealey, Robert................. 25	Naro, Ronald 111
McFarland, Annette C. Miller 108	Meissner, Jack 80, 122	Naro, Veronica D............... 111
McFarland, Beth 93, 109	Michael....................... 2	Nash, Randy 64
McFarland, Bonny Sue 109	Michael, Edna Holcomb 51	Neal, Mrs..................... 96
McFarland, Carol Ann, J.D. ... 108-109	Michael, Ella 86	Neal, Wallace 36
McFarland, Chad L............... 109	Michelsen, Fredrick............. 123	Neet, Albert 51
McFarland, Corley B. (Big Mac).......	Michelsen, Fredrick John 123	Neet, Ancil................... 111
.... 8-9, 24-26, 73, 91, 108-109, 130	Michelsen, Pauline 123	Neet, Anna Lawson 111
McFarland, Corley Wm. 109	Mickey, Rose M. 119	Neet, Art 111
McFarland, Emily A.............. 109	Mikesell, Betty.................. 8	Neet, Daisy Petit 111
McFarland, Harvey John ... 25, 96, 108	Mikesell, Marshall 8	Neet, Dorothy 111
McFarland, Heather Ann 109	Miller, Captain 5	Neet, Esther 111
McFarland, Jean, R.D. 99, 109	Miller, Bessie (Ma) 64	Neet, Ida Fox 111
McFarland, Jenny Lee 109	Miller, Carroll 64	Neet, Joseph 111
McFarland, Joan Townes 109	Miller, Debra 117	Neet, Margaret Carter.......... 111
McFarland, Kirk L............... 109	Miller, Eliris 6	Neet, Ole 111
McFarland, Lee Lowery ... 25, 108-109	Miller, Florence 103	Neet, Rachel 111
McFarland, Mark. L., D.V.M........ 109	Mills, John 71	Neet, Sadie 111
McFarland, Miles P. Miller 108	Minick, Bill.................... 26	Neet, Susan Emaline 125
McFarland, Muriel Walker 108-109	Minkler, Mel................... 63	Neet, Vernon M................ 111
McFarland, Robin 64, 85, 109	Mitchell, Blacketor & Associates... 31	Neet, Vida Walsh 111
McFarland, Ruth Hyland .. 25, 108-109	Moffit, Lawrence 53	Neet, Viola James 111
McFarland, Sally 109	Moisio, Beatrice 121	Neet, Warren 111
McGee, Richard 52	Momb, Malena 51	Nelson, Brenda Joy (Lee) 87
McGill, Artie Zoe................ 87	Montgomery, Darrell............ 110	Nelson, Cleo (Kearns).......... 111
McGillvery, Anna Lindsay 109	Montgomery, Leland 58	Nelson, David 112
McGillvery, Ellen Skidmore 109	Montgomery, Lillie Schieive....... 110	Nelson, Donna................ 128
McGillvery, Ernest 109	Montgomery, Lowell 110	Nelson, Gilbert 57, 111
McGillvery, James 54, 109	Montgomery, Lynette 110, 114	Nelson, Jeri (Pickens) 111
McGillvery, Lillian Ryker 118	Montgomery, Samuel P. 110	Nelson, John 112
McGillvery, William J............. 109	Morgan, C. D. 47	Nelson, Kristie 64
McGuiness, Father Eugene 55	Morgan, Cliff 76	Nelson, Leon (Tyke) 111
McIntire, Rev................... 55	Morris, Addie L. 23-24	Nelson, Louise (Brown)......... 128
McKenzie, Katherine 91	Morris, Blanche 110	Nelson, Maureen 111

Nelson, Mayme 83	Ottinger, Linda 98	Peterson, Elsworth 56
Nelson, Mertel 57	Overland, Wally 130	Peterson, Emily 91
Nelson, Michael 111	Owens, Carla Mae Vaughn 113	Peterson, James A. 91
Nelson, Myrtle 111	Owens, Lawrence Wesley (Wes) 113, 130	Peterson, Robert 66
Nelson, Nadine (Strayer).......... 128	Owens, Monica Leigh 113	Pettijohn, Charlie 36
Nelson, Noell 128	Owens, Wesley Blaine 113	Pettijohn, F. Dolores 116
Nelson, Scott 87	Packard 34	Petit, Daisy 111
Nelson, Tina 112	Paddock, Carrie Lynn 115	Pettit, Ann 54
Neuberger, Richard L............. 19	Paddock, Charles A. ... 13, 58, 63, 114	Pettit, Eddie 54
Neyman, Bessie 117	Paddock, Charles A., Jr. 114	Pettit, Max. 54
Neyman, Elvina 89	Paddock, Charles B. 114	Pflughaupt, Judy 111
Niemi, Francis Wm. (Bill) 112	Paddock, Charles Mathew 115	Phearson, Howard 91
Niemi, George H. 112	Paddock, Charlie............ 11–12, 62	Phearson, Peggy (Crist) 91
Niemi, Harold A. 112	Paddock, Diane (Waddle) 115	Phearson, Vonnie 91
Niemi, Helena Ruth (Bones)....... 112	Paddock, Eleanor (Mrs. Osburn Fisher). 114	Pickens, Jeri..................... 111
Niemi, Janice (Splawn) 112	Paddock, Ella (Beulah) (Worden) ... 114	Poggie, June (Mrs. Ernest) 114
Niemi, Melvin E. 112	Paddock, Etta (Mrs. Virgil Herndon) 114	Pokorny, Charles Anthony 115
Niemi, Roger D. 112	Paddock, Evelyn 114	Pokorny, Francis 115
Niemi, Sheryl (Batson) 112	Paddock, Gordon 114	Pokorny, Olivia 115
Niemi, William M. 112	Paddock, James 63, 114	Pokorny, Sandra M............... 115
Niemi, Wilma Pauline (Paula) 112	Paddock, James (Jim).......... 57, 62	Poole, Dr. Marshall 65–66, 104
Nimocks, Steve 64	Paddock, James, Jr................ 114	Pope & Talbot... 37–39, 41, 47, 49, 63,
Noland, Alvin C. 112	Paddock, Jamie 114	65, 87, 89, 91–92, 96–99, 104, 106–108
Noland, Cleveland 112	Paddock, Jane (Mrs. Ernest Poggie) 114	Powell, Eldon 52
Noland, Daniel A. 112	Paddock, Lynette (Montgomery) ... 114	Powell, Melvin 52
Noland, Donald L. 112	Paddock, Olive (Mrs. Howard Bernhart). 114	Powers, Squire 6
Noland, Doris J. (Swanson) 112	Paddock, Pearl J.................. 114	Praces, Lucille 97
Noland, Elmer D. 112	Paddock, Ronel 63, 114	Preschun, Julie 64
Noland, Gloria D. (Harp) 112	Paddock, Sandra M. 114	Prokop, Clara 51, 94
Noland, Helen M. (Harris) 112	Paddock, Winifred 114	Puckett, Bill 36
Noland, Ian 112	Paddock, Worden 114	Pugh, Flora M................... 89
Noland, Isaac 112	Page, Judy Clark 89	Priddy......................... 88
Noland, Mary Jane 112	Pahle, Kris 83	Priddy, Bruce................... 115
Noland, Melonie 112	Parker 5	Priddy, Elaine (Young) 115
Noland, Peggy (Norris) 112	Parker, Clay 36	Priddy, Joe C. 115
Nordenson, Dave 60	Parker, John 6	Priddy, Mark 115
Nordgren, Judith 113	Parker, Samuel Franklin 104	Priddy, Rebecca 115
Norris, Peggy 112	Parks, Donald Spencer Hughey 104	Prouty, Erin 83
Norris, W. L. 47	Parks, Helen 116	Prouty, Gyneth 8, 64
Oakley, Norman 8	Parks, Kerry Ann Hughey 104	Pugh, Flora M. 89
Obermeyer, Bob 82	Parks, Roy O. 25	Purdy, Van 80
O'Connell, Bob 112	Parvin 5	Purdy, Mrs. Van 80
O'Connell, Eileen 112	Paschelke, Leo 79	Putnam, Alice Salsbury ... 64, 115–116
O'Connell, Franchon 112	Patrick, Alberta 99	Putnam, Carol 115
O'Connell, John 55, 112	Patterson, Governor Paul 88	Putnam, Catherine 115
O'Connell, Mrs. John 55	Pauly, Martha................... 100	Putnam, Irene 116
O'Connell, Larry 112	Payne, Eric 8	Putnam, Janet 115
O'Connell, Tom 112	Pearson, Dorothy................. 90	Putnam, Jay S. 115–116
Odell, W. H. 15, 76	Pearson, Elvina 90	Putnam, Jeanne (Lindsay) 115
O'Hearn, Russell 86	Pearson, Peter 90	Putnam, Kathy 64
O'Hearn, Samantha............... 86	Pedigo, Mary Ryker 118	Putnam, Keith 7
Oleson, Annie 113	Peinecke, Ralph 58	Putnam, Roy 116
Oleson, Betty 107, 113	Pelzel, Beulah 129	Pyles, Sandra 96
Oleson, Judith Nordgren 113	Penasso, Joseph Wm. 110	Rachor, Peggy 83
Oleson, Katy 113	Pengra, Bynon J..................	Racy, Alta Allen 85
Oleson, LeRoy, Jr. 113	...... 14–15, 49, 76, 86, 88, 106, 123–125	Racy, Sharon 83
Oleson, LeRoy, Sr. 113	Pengra, Charlotte Stearns 15	Raines, Mex 36
Oleson, Lindy 113	Pengra, Ella 49, 125	Ramey, Ercle 10, 64, 116
Oleson, Mildred 113	Pengra, Emma Belle 86	Ramey, Ray 88
Olson, Michelle 83	Pengra, Stella 106	Randall, Kenneth 63–66
Orr, John 36	Perigny, Ralph 8	Rardin, Billie (Hatfield)........... 116
Orr, Lucinda Sanford 1, 88, 113	Perigny, Shirleen 57	Rardin, Charlotte (McKinnis) 116
Orr, Richmond 113	Perkins, Debbie 111	Rardin, Ella M. (Jones) 116
Orr, Theresa 1, 95, 113	Perkins, Leslie 88	Rardin, Helen (Parks) 116
Orr, Thomas 1, 95, 113	Pertuska, Becky 83	Rardin, Hortense Sheffield 116
Orr, Wayne E. 25	Peterson, Alan 91	Rardin, Jack 36
Osborn, Viola 95	Peterson, Ann 56	Rardin, N. James................ 116
Oskay, Billy 8	Peterson, Diane 91	Rardin, Ruth (Churan) 116

Rardin, Thomas (Jack) 116
Rardin, William J. 116
Rasmussan, Susan 93
Ray, Frederick 60
Ray, Jim 67
Ray, Josephine 66
Raymond, Sara Edna 95
Ream, Joanna F. Dunning 116
Ream, Michael Ralph 116
Ream, Ralph Clinton 116
Ream, Terry Joe 116
Reardon, William 26
Redding, Donna................... 8
Redmond, Arion 64
Reed, Dorothy 48
Reed, Janice Tomlin 116
Reed, Jeffrey 116
Reed, Mika Suzanne 116
Reed, Russel 116
Reed, Susan Sanford 1
Reid 88
Reindollar, Ann Jeanette, M.D. 92
Reindollar, Richard, M.D. 92
Rettinger, Kyle Lane 104
Reynolds, Elmira 49
Reynolds, Irene 123
Ricks, Vernon "Cap" 62, 104
Riddle, George 75
Ridenour, Trudy 66
Rigdon, Steve 2
Rigdon, Mrs. 84
Ritchie, George 43
Ritz, Beth Ann 100
Ritz, Neil 100
Ritz, Norman 100
Ritz, Reece 100
Robb, Leo 64
Roberts, Amanda 117
Roberts, Bessie Neyman 117
Roberts, Carol J. 117
Roberts, Chad 117
Roberts, Charles O. 116
Roberts, Cherri Kloster 117
Roberts, Christy D. 117
Roberts, Debra Miller 117
Roberts, Dustin 117
Roberts, Edgar N. (Eddie) .. 36, 64, 116
Roberts, F. Dolores 116
Roberts, Genie Spenser 116
Roberts, Gerald G................ 117
Roberts, James 116–117
Roberts, James H. 117
Roberts, John E. 117
Roberts, Kari 117
Roberts, Kate 117
Roberts, Larry 68
Roberts, Larry D. 117
Roberts, Lyndi 117
Roberts, Michail 117
Roberts, Nathan 117
Roberts, Patti Bergman Denny 117
Roberts, Peter 116
Roberts, Rebecca Wright 117
Roberts, Rosalie Zaln 117
Roberts, Staci 116
Roberts, Steward 117
Roberts, Terry M. 117
Roberts, Thomas 117

Roberts, William D. 117
Robertson, Minnie E. 108
Robinett, Volney 108
Robinson, Mrs. L. J. 47
Rockwell, Audrey Haskett 64, 117
Rockwell, Charles, Jr. 117
Rockwell, Charles Lee 117
Rockwell, Erik 117
Rockwell, Gay Butler 117
Rockwell, Marjorie 117
Rockwell, Ryan 117
Rockwell, Tiffany 117
Rockwell, Todd 117
Rodgers, Alva 54
Rodgers, Wanda 54
Rogers, Arden 117
Rogers, Calvin 117
Rogers, Cleone (Bain) 117
Rogers, Inez Flock 64, 117
Rogers, Jim 36
Rogers, Luke 36
Rogers, Luther E. 71, 117
Rogers, Lyle 117
Rogers, Oral 117
Rogers, Tamaris (Clifford) 90, 117
Rogers, Sharon (Kirby) 117
Rogers, Tracy 117
Ross, Bill 36
Roth, Katherine 119
Rue, Al 63
Runyon, Ray 54
Russell, Dee 35
Russell, Hal 35
Russell, Kathleen 51
Russell, T. O. 47
Ruth, R. Laura 51
Rutherford, Genevieve Eaton 94
Ryan, M. 14–15
Ryan, Thomas 23–24
Ryker, Clarence A. 118
Ryker, Edith (Brown) 118
Ryker, Edna (Temple) 50, 118, 122
Ryker, Erma Jean 45
Ryker, John Augustus 118
Ryker, John J. 45
Ryker, Katherine 50
Ryker, Lillian (McGillvery) 50, 118
Ryker, Louis S. 64, 118
Ryker, Mamie (Eskridge) 118
Ryker, Manie D. Williams 118
Ryker, Mary (Pedigo) 118
Ryker, Myrtis (Wojcik) 118
Ryman, Ben 118
Ryman, Phyllis (Sorensen) . 48, 118–119
Safle, Wayne 43
Sageras, Clara Stiers 52
Salsbury, Alice 115
Salsbury, Arthur H. 115
Salsbury, Donna 115
Salsbury, Gayle 115
Sanchez, Ben 66
Sanford, Gordon S. 25
Sanford, James ....
.... 1–2, 26, 45, 100, 113, 118
Sanford, Josiah 1, 118
Sanford, Lucinda (Orr) 1, 118
Sanford, Richmond 1, 2, 118
Sanford, Susan (Reed) 1

Sankey, Fred R. 12
Sassaman, Raymond 66
Sayre, Andru 118
Sayre, Colleen Evers 118
Sayre, Doris I. Walker........... 118
Sayre, Karen Lynn............... 118
Sayre, Lacy H. 118
Sayre, Mathew 118
Sayre, Michelle 118
Sayre, Robert F. 118
Schafer, Marissa Renee 102
Schafer, Mikaela Kristine 102
Schafer, Ramona Reed 102
Schiewe, Lillie 110
Schmidt, Barbara 56, 103
Schmidt, Claude 56
Schmidt, Gerald 56
Schmidt, Mildred 56
Schmidt, Ronald 56
Schneider, Mark 8
Schroeder, Sandy 8
Schwebke, Cris 48
Schwebke, Mark 68
Scroggins, Arthur 58
Searle, Gary (Joe) 7
Sears, Major 73
Sears, Opal 106
Shackleford, Wesley 36
Shamek, Gene 8
Sharp & Michael's 2
Sharp, Bill 128
Sharp, Cherriet 128
Sharp, Darren 128
Sharp, Elizabeth (Beth) 128
Sharp, Jacqueline (Armstrong)..... 128
Sharp, James 128
Sharp, Jennifer 128
Sharp, Laura 51–52, 95
Sharp, Mary Beth 128
Sharp, Walter 128
Shedd, Gertrude 106
Sheffield, Hortense 116
Shelley 45
Sherman, Beverly Stafford 118
Sherman, C. Avery 118
Sherman, Francis Lamonte 118
Sherman, Louis Avery 118
Sherman, Mildred Flock 118
Sherman, Mildred Lenore Vanderpool 118
Shimmin, Robert 47
Shorey, Brothers 88
Siefken, Esther 52
Sietz, Clyde 74
Simon 88
Simpson, Lynn 64
Sims, Ann Marie (Bloom) 119
Sims, Cathy L. (Lobben) 119
Sims, Genevieve M. (Brewer) .. 87, 119
Sims, John P. 119
Sims, Paul M. 119
Sims, Rose 48, 119
Singletary, Ethel 98–99
Singletary, Georgie 58
Singletary, John 99
Singletary, Mr. 13
Sittser, Adrain D. 69
Sittser, Ernest 58
Sittser, Esther Beach 69

Name	Page
Sittser, G. G. (Gerry)	68
Sittser, Kathleen G.	69
Sittser, Laura Lee	69
Sittser, Rodney E.	69
Skaar, Garth	8
Skeens, Wibby	64
Skidmore, Ellen McGillvrey	109
Skinner, Eugene	47, 101
Skinner, Mrs. Eugene	113
Skoubo, Jannel	111
Skoubo, Kathy	111
Smith, Cheryl	8
Smith, E. E.	2
Smith, Gladys	50
Smith, Mack	54
Smith, Mary	101
Smith, Quentin	67
Smith, Salli	121
(The) Smothers Brothers	126
Snuggerud, Cris	8
Snuggerud, Ross	64
Snyder, John	43
Sorensen, Barbara (Bobbie) (McMahon)	109, 119
Sorensen, Ina Ann Woodward	110
Sorensen, Joseph	119
Sorensen, Margaret (McAtee, Long)	119
Sorensen, Marion	119
Sorensen, William (Bill)	110, 119
Sorseth, Alvin	25
Spalinger, Albert	119–120
Spalinger, Alvin	119
Spalinger, Edwin	119
Spalinger, Herman	119
Spalinger, John	119
Spalinger, Katherine Roth	119–120
Spalinger, Katherine Elizabeth (Betty)	119
Spalinger, Lois Walker	119
Spalinger, Martin (Bim)	119, 125
Spalinger, Melvin	119
Spatz, Kay	41
Spatz, Melvin	41
Spellmire, Jean	48
Spencer, Anna Marie	104
Spencer, Doty	7, 64
Spencer, Rachel	7–8
Spenser, Genie	116
Splawn, Janice	112
Sprague, Gilbert	96
Stafford, A. E.	63
Stafford, Beverly Jean	118
Stalcup, Laura	63
Staley, Virginia	64
Staley, W. F.	76
Starbird, Captain	28
Starkbien, Judith (Mrs. Kenneth)	105
Starr, Alma	48
Starr, Ross	48
Stears, Nancy	91
Stein, Henry	105
Stephens, Edna	51
Stephens, Joyce	53
Stephens, Richard	58
Stevens, Christy	127
Stevens, Kathlyn Louise	127
Stevens, Lloyd W.	127
Stevenson	5
Stewart, Agnes	5, 55, 125–126
Stewart, Elizabeth	126
Stewart, Fanny	51
Stewart, Jessie	101
Stewart, John	5, 55
Stewart, Loran L. (Stub)	37–38, 42–43, 89, 130
Stewart, Mary	126
Stewart, Mrs.	48
Stichell, Trent	67
Stiers, Sid	52
Stiffy, Josephine	105
Stillwell, Ellen	123
Stockton, Everett	54
Stone, Norman	31
Stone, Sheryl	64
Stonebreaker, Myrtle	52
Stonebreaker, Richard	52
Stoukey, Betty	120
Stoukey, Florence Holt	120
Stoukey, Maxine	120
Stoukey, Percy	120
Stout, Julie	83
Strakbein, Edna M.	109
Straub, Robert	62
Strayer, Nadine	128
Streit, Carole	121
Streit, Ella (Tuchardt)	120–121, 126
Streit, Helen	121, 126
Streit, Kellie (Murray)	121
Streit, Louis (Louie)	55, 120–121, 126
Streit, Marla (Ciesiel)	121
Streit, Richard W.	121
Streit, Robert	121
Streit, Ruth (Lovelady)	121
Streit, Salli (Smith)	121
Streit, Scott	121
Sullivan, Kelly	74
Sutherlin, Olive	89
Sutton, W. G.	55
Svendsen, Charles W.	121
Svendsen, Cheryl Ann	121
Svendsen, Christian	121
Svendsen, Karen Lynn	121
Svendsen, Nancy Ann Johnson	121
Svendsen, Richard A.	121
Svendsen, Susan Lennox	121
Svendsen, Wilfred O.	121
Svendsen, Wilma Mays	121
Swank, Barbara	121
Swank, Cathy	122
Swank, Christine	122
Swank, David	122
Swank, Doris	122
Swank, Elizabeth	121
Swank, Evelyn Lindke	121
Swank, Harry	121
Swank, Harry E.	121–122
Swank, Jeanne	121
Swank, Joanna	122
Swank, Josephine	122
Swank, Patricia	122
Swank, Robert	121–122
Swanson, Doris	112
Swanson, Freddy	52
Swanson, Jeffery	100
Swanson, Joshua	100
Swanson, Rod	100
Swanson, Susan Kay	100
Swaryck, Ann Allen	85
Sybouts, Ward	64
Tabor, Bryan	97
Tabor, Heather	97
Tabor, Mike	97
Tabor, Tammy	97
Tatro, Barbara	89
Taylor, Darlinda (Suzie)	103
Taylor, Dave	56
Taylor, Joe	76
Taylor, Mary Kathryn	99
Temple, Diane Dooley	122
Temple, Don	122
Temple, Edna Ryker	8, 18, 64, 80, 118, 122
Temple, Greta	122
Temple, Roy	64, 80, 122
Temple, Shirley	122
Templeman, E. T.	1, 8–9
Templeman, Eldon	63
Thatcher, George	71, 123
Thatcher, Irene	123
Thomas, Brian	100
Thomas, Jeannie	65
Thomas, Jocelyn	100
Thomas, Lincoln	100
Thomas, Mary Alice	100
Thomas, Tommy	65
Thomen, Claire	91
Thompson, Debbie	83
Thompson, Dewayne	54
Thompson, Edna	56
Thurman, Naomi Allen	85
Tiller, Clara	122
Tiller, Dale Leroy	122
Tiller, Daphne	8
Tiller, Darlene Faye (Lister)	122
Tiller, Donald Roy	122
Tiller, Dustin	8
Tiller, Ermal Aaron	122
Tiller, Hazel	108, 122
Tiller, Hazel M.	122
Tiller, Jesse	122
Tiller, Karon	8
Tiller, Larry Gene	122
Tiller, Mary Ellen (Ella) Flock	95, 122
Tiller, Nadine Evelyn (Lunyou)	122
Tiller, Nancy Marie	122
Tiller, Rachel	122
Tiller, Patsy Joan (Gilliam)	122
Tiller, Paul	8
Tiller, Paul Allen	122
Tiller, Sherman William	122
Tiller, Thomas Jefferson	122
Tiller, Thurmon	122
Tiller, Verna May (Loudermilk)	122
Tiller, Wes	8
Tiller, Wesley Ermal	122
Tilley, Alyson Blair	93
Tilley, Karen Diess	93
Tilley, Kirk John	93
Tillotson, Bobby	89
Tillotson, Christine	89
Tiner, Siegle	52
Tonsgard, Elizabeth	8
Tonsgard, Nomi	8
Torgeson, Patti	111
Torrence, Carol	123
Towne, Howard	36

Townes, Joan 109
Tracy, Brad...................... 123
Tracy, Ellen Stillwell 123
Tracy, Irene Reynolds 123
Tracy, Robert E., Jr. 123
Tracy, Robert (Bob) E., Sr. 16, 123
Tracy, Shannon 123
Tracy, Shirley B. (Jowers)..... 105, 123
Trentz, Betsy 111
Tuchardt, Anna 56
Tuchardt, Charles 56
Tuchardt, Dale 52
Tuchardt, Ella 120
Tuchardt, Emma 56
Tuchardt, Frances 56
Tuchardt, Henry 56
Tuchardt, Herbert 56
Tuchardt, Leah 56
Tuchardt, William, Jr. 56
Tuchardt, William, Sr. 56
Tufti, Charlie .. 3, 76, 94, 108, 125, 130
Tufti, Lucy 3
Tomlin, Audrey Koskey (Randle) ... 122
Tomlin, Betty (Johnson) 122
Tomlin, Carol (Torrence).......... 123
Tomlin, Chris E.................. 122
Tomlin, Deanna D. 123
Tomlin, Devon M. 123
Tomlin, Dwane 123
Tomlin, Gene 122
Tomlin, Janice 116
Tomlin, Lori................ 110, 122
Tomlin, Louise Chambers......... 122
Tomlin, Mark D. 123
Tomlin, N. Sam 122
Tripp, Carol J. 117
Tripp, Diane 117
Tripp, Kristopher 117
Tripp, Warren 117
Triplett, Mary Ellen............... 129
Troth, Sadie 111
Truelove, Christy D. 117
Truelove, Kelli 117
Truelove, Robin 117
Truelove, Valaria 117
Trumbull, Willard 82
Tucker, Mrs. Cecil 56
Tucker, Max 37
Tullock, Freddie, R.N. 64–65
Tullock, Julie Myroene 123
Tullock, Myron Budge 123
Tullock, Pauline Fredrickson, R.N. . 123
Tupper, W. L. (Bill) 16
Tveit, Carmen Lee................ 123
Tveit, E. Mildred 123
Tveit, Evelyn Mildred McMahon ... 123
Tveit, Lavon 123
Tweedy 98
Tyler, Dr......................... 65
Tyler, Frank 65
Undi, Stanley 25
Upmeyer, Heidi 83
Vanderpool, Mildred Lenore 118
Van Natta, Rev. Tim 57, 64
Van Vleet, Hattie 50
Varney, Dr. George C. 65, 104, 123
Varney, Mrs..................... 66
Vaughn, Carla Mae 113

Vaughn, Gary 122
Vaughn, Kim 122
Vaughn, Patric Scott 122
Vearnier, Hazel 98
Vearnier, M. C. "Bud"............ 98
Velasco, Dorothy 7
Vincent, Mary 104
Vonderheit...................... 105
Waddle, Diane 115
Wade, Louise 7
Walborn, Marge................... 8
Waldo, Edith 84
Waldo, Judge John B. 84
Waldorf, Lou 79
Walker, Ansel.................... 97
Walker, Bessie Louise 125
Walker, Betty (Spalinger) 119
Walker, Carl A. 54
Walker, Donald E., Sr. 36, 45, 118–119, 124
Walker, Donald E., Jr............. 125
Walker, Doris Irene 118, 124
Walker, Ella Pengra 107, 123, 125
Walker, Elsie G. 125
Walker, Grace Hills.................
.... 35, 47, 51, 101, 118, 124
Walker, James A. 107, 123, 125
Walker, James A. (Mrs.) 86
Walker, James Elwin 124
Walker, Larry A. 125
Walker, Lois W. 119, 125
Walker, Louise (Clark) 50, 88, 125
Walker, Muriel 108
Walker, Olive May Gray.... 88, 95, 125
Walker, Samuel Earl...............
.... 36, 45, 47, 58, 123–125
Walker, Thelma Carter 125
Walker, Wayne V. 125
Walker, William S. .. 45, 47, 88, 95, 125
Walsh, Vida 111
Warfield, Mrs. B. B. 81
Warfield, Phoebe 100
Warner........................ 5–6
Warner, Agnes Stewart .. 104, 125–126
Warner, Belle 47
Warner, Elizabeth (McDowell) 125
Warner, Elizabeth Stewart 74–75, 125–126
Warner, F. A. 76
Warner, Flora 12, 49
Warner, Flora (Dompier) 125
Warner, Frank 3, 12, 47, 55, 76, 78, 94, 125
Warner, Mrs. Frank 55
Warner, Fred......... 73, 75, 125–126
Warner, George 105, 125
Warner, Isabelle (Abrams) 125
Warner, John 126
Warner, Lina (Flock) 94, 125
Warner, Susan 125
Warner, Susan Emaline Neet 125
Warner, Thomas 125–126
Warner, Tom 104–105
Warner, Tracy 105, 125
Warner, Vina 125
Warren, A. L. 25
Washburn, Gary 58
Watson, W. T..................... 47
Weaver, Velma 97
Webb, Carl, Jr. 54
Weddle, Larry 56

Wegge, Judy 102
Welborn, Pat 83
Wells, Patricia 90
Wert, Elizabeth 92
Wessner, Vesta................... 56
West, Patricia Ann 85, 123
West, Robert Edward 123
West, Williams F.................. 123
Wester, Carl 31
Wheeler 37
Whitaker, Jim 36
Whitaker, Sondra................ 105
White, Barbara 126
White, Candy 8
White, Carla 126
White, Clifford E. 126
White, David 8
White, Helen (Streit) 126
White, Kenneth 126
Whittaker, Mrs. F. 55
Wick, Herb 25
Wick, Sharon 57
Wilcox, Harriet 108
Wilcox, Henry, Jr. 54
Wilcox, Leona Blakely 86
Wilcox, Nancy 83
Wilcox, Wendy 83
Wiley, I. I. 47
Wilhelm, Wes.................... 36
Wilkinson, Jack 66
Willey, Carol (Lenocher).......... 126
Willey, George R. 126
Willey, James 126
Willey, Mary V. (Bowyer) 126
Willey, Melvin 126
Willey, Thelma (Barnes) 126
Williams, Charley 5
Williams, Charlie 35
Williams, Cleo 98
Williams, Edith 63
Williams, Lillian 64
Williams, Manie D. 118
Williams, Mason D. .. 7–8, 87, 126–127
Williams, Velma Luella 89
Williams, Vern 104
Williams, Willard 98
Williamson, Gary 64
Wilson, Merton 63
Wilson, Dr. O. Meredith 90
Wilson, Woodrow 124
Winfrey, Carrie 127
Winfrey, Cora 45
Winfrey, Dan 52
Winfrey, Daniel R. 127
Winfrey, Percey 45
Winfrey, W. E. 127
Winfrey, Wilbur 34, 51
Winkelman, Eva Mae 106
Winkelman, Hattie 106
Winkelman, Iva 106
Winkelman, Virgil 106
Winkelman, Virgil, Jr. 106
Winkelman, Williams (Harry) 106
Winn, Sam 80
Wiser, Elizabeth Hendershott 127
Wiser, James 127
Wiser, James E. (Jim) 127
Wiser, Janice (Henning) 127

Wojcik, Myrtis 118	Woodruff, Leota (Zander) 128	Worth, Veryl M. 7, 32, 129
Wolf, Alta 51	Woodruff, Lois Goforth 128	Wright, Beulah 129
Wolf, Altadena 128	Woodruff, Michael Allen 128	Wright, Charles Walter 129
Wolf, Arthur 47, 128	Woodruff, Oral Allen 128	Wright, Dee 74
Wolf, Bertha (Hadley) 128	Woodruff, Rick 128	Wright, Florence Elizabeth 129
Wolf, Boy A. 128	Woodruff, Vaughn (Ike) 128	Wright, Jack 41
Wolf, Boyd 51	Woodward, Dr. Emmit 65	Wright, Jacob Charles 129
Wolf, Pearl 51, 128	Woodward, Ina Ann 119	Wright, Max 65
Wolf, Rose (Condon) 128	Woods, Richard 43	Wright, Minnie B. Madaris 41, 129
Wolf, Susan Burchard 128	Woods, Trisha 83	Wright, Rebecca 117
Wolf, W. H. 47	Woods, W. 108	Yeager 88
Wolf, William Henry 128	Woolery, Karen 93	Young, Baxter 108
Wood, Anna Durkee 128	Wooley, Lewis Scott 129	Young, Brown & Young 36
Wood, Arch 2, 49, 128	Woolfolk, Doris 91	Young, Elaine 115
Wood, Maurice 128	Woolridge, Beverly 31	Young, Jim 64
Woodard, Myron 29	Woolridge, Lee 64	Yunk, Joseph 55
Woodruff, Cherriet (Karnes) 128	Worden, Beulah 12	Zaln, Rosalie 117
Woodruff, Dane 128	Worden, Ella Beulah 114	Zander, Leota 128
Woodruff, Donna 128	Worth, Franklin S. 129	Z'berg, Vicki 93
Woodruff, Elizabeth (Beth) 128	Worth, Harry S. 7, 63–64, 129	Zevely, C. H. 50–51
Woodruff, Heral (Woody) A. 128	Worth, Mary Ellen Triplett 129	Zevely, Mrs. C. H. 51
Woodruff, Janis (Hancock) 128	Worth, Susan McCorkell R. D. 129